PIANO • VOCAL • GUITAR

NATIONAL ANTHEMS
FROM AROUND THE WORLD

*The Official National Anthems, Flags,
and Anthem Histories from 56 Countries*

ISBN 0-7935-6079-9

HAL•LEONARD™
CORPORATION
7777 W. BLUEMOUND RD. P.O. BOX 13819 MILWAUKEE, WI 53213

THE COUNTRIES AND THEIR NATIONAL ANTHEMS

18	Australia	*Advance Australia Fair*
20	Austria	*Land der Berge, Land am Strome*
22	Bahamas	*March On, Bahamaland!*
25	Barbados	*In Plenty And In Time Of Need*
28	Belize	*O Land Of The Free*
36	Bolivia	*Bolivianos, el hado propicio*
40	Brazil	*Ouviram do Ipirangas as margens placidas*
44	Canada	*O Canada!*
31	Chile	*Puro Chile es tu cielo azulado*
46	Colombia	*¡Oh gloria inmarcesible!*
50	Costa Rica	*Noble patria*
54	Cuba	*La bayamesa*
56	Czech Republic	*Kde Domov Můj?*
58	Dominican Republic	*Quisqueyanos valientes, alcemos*
62	Ecuador	*¡Salve, oh patria, mil veces!*
64	El Salvador	*Saludemos la patria orgullosos*
68	Estonia	*Mu isamaa, mu õnn ja rõõm*
70	Finland	*Maamme*
72	France	*La Marseillaise*
78	Germany	*Einigkeit und Recht und Freiheit*
80	Great Britain	*God Save The Queen*
84	Greece	*Segnorizo apo tin kopsi*
86	Grenada	*Hail! Grenada, Land Of Ours*
75	Guatemala	*¡Guatemala feliz!*
88	Haiti	*La Dessalinienne*
90	Honduras	*Tu bandera, tu bandera un lampo de cielo*
94	Irish Republic	*Amhrán na bhFiann*

96	Israel	*Hatiqvah*
81	Italy	*Inno di Mameli*
98	Jamaica	*Eternal Father, Bless Our Land*
100	Japan	*Kimigayo*
104	Latvia	*Dievs Seveti Latviju*
101	Liberia	*All Hail, Liberia, Hail!*
106	Mexico	*Mexicanos, al grito de guerra*
110	New Zealand	*God Defend New Zealand*
112	Nicaragua	*Salve a tí Nicaragua*
114	North Korea (Korean Democratic People's Republic)	*Ach'im ûn pinnara*
116	Norway	*Ja, vi elsker*
118	Panama	*Himno Istmeño*
126	Paraguay	*A los pueblos*
121	Peru	*¡Somos Libres!*
130	Philippines	*Bayang Magiliw*
132	Poland	*Jeszcze Polska nie zginęla*
134	Russia	*from A Life For The Czar*
136	Slovakia	*Nad Tatrou Sa Blyska*
138	South Africa	*Die Stem van Suid-Afrika*
142	South Korea (Korean Republic)	*Tonghai moolkwa Paiktusani*
144	Spain	*Marcha real*
148	Sweden	*Du gamla, du fria*
145	Switzerland	*Swiss Psalm*
150	Uganda	*Pearl Of Africa*
152	Ukraine	*Shche ne vmerla Ukrania*
154	United States of America	*The Star-Spangled Banner*
157	Uruguay	*¡Orientales, la patria o la tumba!*
164	Venezuela	*Gloria al bravo pueblo*
162	Vietnam	*Tiên quân ca*

THE ANTHEMS

AUSTRALIA
Advance Australia Fair

Until 1974 Australia's official national anthem was *God Save The Queen.* In 1973 a competition was held to select a new anthem. Thousands of entries were received but none of them met with the judges' approval. Subsequently several public opinion polls were held to see which of Australia's three most popular patriotic songs should become the national anthem: *Advance Australia Fair* (words and music by Peter Dodds McCormick alias *Amicus*); *Waltzing Matilda* (words by Andrew Barton "Banjo" Paterson, music a traditional Scottish melody); or *God Save The Queen. Advance Australia Fair* easily defeated the other two songs by receiving almost three million votes. On April 19, 1974 *Advance Australia Fair* was officially declared Australia's national anthem.

AUSTRIA
Land der Berge, Land am Strome

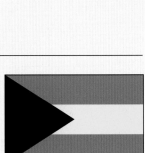

Prior to World War II the melody to the Austrian national anthem was the Franz Joseph Haydn (1732-1809) tune taken from his *Emperor Quartet* (Op. 76, no. 3). The Nazis appropriated this tune for *Deutschland, Deutschland über Alles* during World War II. Because of the connotations that became attached to this song, Austria changed its anthem immediately after World War II.

Traditionally the melody to the new *Österreichische Bundeshymne* (Austrian National Hymn) has been attributed to Wolfgang Amadeus Mozart (1756-1791) although Austrian scholars cite more evidence to favor Johann Holzer as the composer. The lyrics were written by the poet Paula Preradović (1887-1951) and were adopted as the *Österreichische Bundeshymne* in 1947.

BAHAMAS
March On, Bahamaland!

The government of the Bahamas selected and approved this anthem submitted by Timothy Gibson (born 1903) in a national competition completed on November 21, 1972. It did not become the official anthem until July 10, 1973 upon declaration of independence from Britain. On this date the Bahamas officially became the thirty-third member of The Commonwealth of Nations.

BARBADOS
In Plenty And In Time Of Need

While under formal British rule, *God Save The Queen* was the national anthem of Barbados. The current anthem was adopted on November 30, 1966 when the country declared independence and became part of The Commonwealth of Nations.

BELIZE
O Land Of The Free

Formerly called British Honduras, Belize became an independent member of The Commonwealth of Nations on September 21, 1981. A new national anthem was adopted on Independence Day even though the British maintained troops in the country as a defense force against Guatemala, which refused to recognize Belize as an independent state.

BOLIVIA
Bolivianos, el hado propicio

Bolivia is named after Simon Bolivar (1783-1864), a Venezuelan patriot whose fight against Spanish reign in South America secured him the title *El Liberator*. *Bolivianos, el hado propicio* (Bolivians, Kind Fate) was adopted as the national anthem of the República de Bolivia in 1845. José Ignacio de Sanjinés (1786-1864), a signer of Bolivia's declaration of independence and its first constitution, penned the lyrics in 1825. The music was created by the Italian composer L. Benedetto Vincenti.

BRAZIL
Ouviram do Ipirangas as margens placidas

To celebrate the coronation in 1831 of Emperor Don Pedro II a new national anthem was composed by Francisco Manoel da Silva, court composer and founder of the National Conservatory and the Philharmonic Orchestra in Rio de Janeiro. In 1889 Brazil became a republic and held an unsuccessful competition to find a completely new anthem. The poem *Ouviram do Ipirangas as margens placidas* (A Cry Rang Out From Peaceful Ipiranga's Banks) by Joaquim Osório Duque Estrada was eventually chosen to replace the original anonymous text. This combination of text and music was officially adopted as the Republic's national anthem in 1922.

CANADA
O Canada!

In 1880 a few prominent members of French-Canadian patriotic society requested Calixa Lavallée to set the French text *O Canada* to music. At that time Lavallée was a highly respected musical figure in both Canada and the United States, occupying the position of Director of the Grand Opera House in New York (later to become the Metropolitan Opera House). The English lyrics by Robert Stanley Weir is not a translation of the French but is a completely new text.

God Save The Queen has maintained status as the royal anthem used for occasions associated with the monarchy of England.

CHILE
Puro Chile es tu cielo azulado

Chile's first national anthem was written in 1819 following the eight-year war of independence from Spain (1810-1818) which had been led by the patriots José de San Martin and Bernardo O'Higgins. A new musical setting of the first text was composed by Ramón Carnicer in 1828. After a peace treaty between Spain and Chile was signed in 1847, Eusebio Lillo was commissioned to write a new text less bitter toward Spain. The present text was officially adopted on June 27, 1941.

COLOMBIA
¡Oh gloria inmarcesible!

In addition to writing the text to *¡Oh gloria inmarcesible!* Rafael Núñez (1825-1894) was a prominent political figure who was elected President four times between 1880 and 1888. The composer Orestes Sindici (1837-1904) was a tenor who traveled to Colombia with an Italian opera company and elected to remain.

COSTA RICA
Noble patria

Anecdotal evidence suggests an amusing story behind the composition of the music to the Costa Rican anthem. In 1853 Costa Rica hosted dignitaries from the United States and Britain. As part of the opening ceremony the president was determined that the visitors should be greeted with the Costa Rican national anthem; however, at the time Costa Rica did not have a national anthem. Manuel María Gutiérrez, considered the foremost musician of his day, was ordered to compose an anthem. He protested that he was a performer, not a composer. This did not deter the president, who ordered Gutiérrez imprisoned until he wrote an appropriate song. This imprisonment resulted in the music which was adopted in 1853. The text by José María Zeledón Brenes (1877-1949) was selected as the result of a competition held in 1900.

CUBA
La bayamesa

The Cuban national anthem is referred to as *La bayamesa* since it commemorates the Battle of Bayamo fought in 1868 against Spanish rule. Pedro Figueredo, both lyricist and composer of this anthem, was a commander of the revolutionary forces during this battle. His inspiration came from witnessing the storming of the village of Guanabacoa by Spanish forces. Figueredo was ultimately captured in 1870 by the Spanish army and executed by a firing squad.

CZECH REPUBLIC
Kde Domov Můj?

Prior to January 1, 1993 the Czech and Slovak nations were united in a federation. Performance of their national anthems, done consecutively, formed a "protest" song against foreign rule. With the creation of the new Czech and Slovak Republics the anthems were divided.

The music of the Czech national anthem was taken from Frantisek Jan Skroup's operetta *Shoemaker's Fair* (1834) with lyrics by Josef Kajetán Tyl. It was officially adopted in 1919. Performance is traditionally done by a symphony orchestra, without a professional singer. Only on rare, emotional occasions will the audience sing.

DOMINICAN REPUBLIC
Quisqueyanos valientes, alcemos

Quisqueyanos valientes, alcemos (Brave Men Of Quisqueya, Let Us Raise Our Song) was composed in 1883 and first sung as the national anthem in 1900. *Quisqueya* is the indigenous name for the island of Santo Domingo.

ECUADOR
¡Salve, oh patria, mil veces!

Napolean's invasion of Spain enabled Ecuador to end three hundred years of Spanish domination. The first Ecuadorian Congress declared independence on December 11, 1811, but Spain was not completely defeated until May 24, 1822 at a battle fought in the foothills near Quito. Composed by Antonio Neumane, with a text by Juan León Mera, *¡Salve, oh patria, mil veces!* (May Thy Freedom Be Guarded) was not adopted officially as national anthem until 1948, although it had been in use since 1885.

EL SALVADOR
Saludemos la patria orgullosos

Juan Aberle immigrated to El Salvador in 1845, where he became a renowned music teacher in both Guatemala and El Salvador. He composed *Saludemos la patria orgullosos* (Let Us Proudly Salute Our Country) in 1879, although it was not officially adopted until 1953. The author of the text, General Juan José Cañas (1826-1912), was a soldier, diplomat, and ultimately his country's Minister of Foreign Affairs.

ESTONIA
Mu isamaa, mu õnn ja rõõm

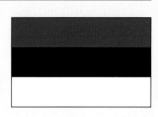

Johann Woldemar Janssen appropriated the melody to *Mu isamaa, mu õnn ja rõõm* (My Native Land, My Pride And Joy) from the Finnish national anthem *Maamme*. *Maamme* was composed in 1848 by Fredrik Pacius (1809-1891). The premiere performance of *Mu isamaa, mu õnn ja rõõm* was given at the First Estonian National Song Festival in Tartu on July 1, 1869. Official adoption as the national anthem did not occur until about 1917, although it was acknowledged as the Eesti Hümn (Estonian National Anthem) since its debut.

FINLAND
Maamme

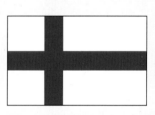

Finland's national poet, Johan Ludvig Runeberg (1804-1877), wrote the poem *Värt land* in 1846. Originally written in Swedish, the poet Paavo Kajander subsequently translated it into Finnish. Composer Fredrik Pacius (1809-1891) was born in Germany but lived most of his life in Helsinski. As founder of the Finnish National School of Music he is recognized as the "Father of Finnish Music." Because Russia ruled Finland for most of the nineteenth century, this anthem became an important patriotic symbol of hope and freedom for the Finnish people.

FRANCE
La Marseillaise

Commissioned by the mayor of Strasbourg to write a marching song for French troops, Captain Claude-Joseph Rouget de L'isle (1760-1836) composed *La Marseillaise* on April 24, 1792 in a single night. Although composed by an army engineer, *La Marseillaise* has become one of the world's best known national anthems. It was originally published as *Chant de guerre pour l'armiée du Rhin* (War Song Of The Army Of The Rhine) since it was sung during the French campaign against Austria. The following June, a company of volunteers sang the song as they entered Paris from Marseilles. The Parisians bestowed the title *La Marseillaise* to the rousing music. Three years later the hastily composed march was officially adopted as France's national anthem. During the Second Empire (1852-1870) a less revolutionary anthem was used, but *La Marseillaise* was reinstated as the national anthem of the *République Francaise* in 1871.

GERMANY
Einigkeit und Recht und Freiheit

German poet August Heinrich Hoffmann von Fallersleben (1798-1874) wrote the text for *Einigkeit und Recht und Freiheit* (Unity And Right And Freedom) in 1841, drawing his inspiration from a poem by the *minnesinger* Walther von der Vogelweide (c1170-1230). In 1841 Germany was made up of more than 30 small states which had been loosely united as the *Deutscher Bund* (German Federation) since 1815. In 1922 the first President of the German Republic officially declared *Einigkeit und Recht und Freiheit* as its *Deutschland-Lied* or national anthem, replacing *Heil Dir im Siegerkranz* which used the melody of *God Save The Queen*. The melody to *Einigkeit und Recht und Freiheit* was written in 1797 by the famous composer Franz Joseph Haydn (1732-1809). This beautiful melody was also used as the national anthem of Austria until 1947 when they adopted a new anthem.

GREAT BRITAIN
God Save The Queen

God Save The Queen is arguably the most famous of all national anthems. It was premiered in its present form on September 28, 1745 as a show of support for King George II. The army of Prince Charles Edward Stewart, the "Young Pretender," had defeated the British army at Prestonpans, Scotland earlier that month. News of this defeat shocked London and an outbreak of patriotic zeal against the new Jacobite threat rallied the people in support of King George II. Thomas Arne (1710-1778), composer of *Rule Brittania* and conductor of the orchestra at the Theatre Royal at Drury Lane, hurriedly arranged the anonymous tune of *God Save The Queen* for soloists and chorus. This arrangement was intended to be performed once in homage to King George II, but its astounding success caused it to be performed nightly at the Theatre Royal.

This anthem has functioned at various times as the national anthem for Denmark, Sweden, Switzerland, Russia, the United States and several independent German states.

GREECE
Segnorizo apo tin kopsi

With one hundred and fifty-eight verses, the text to *Segnorizo apo tin kopsi tou spathiou tin tromeri* (I Shall Always Know You By The Fire In Your Eyes) has the distinction of being the longest national anthem. The poem by Dionysius Solomos (1798-1857) chronicles heroic deeds and battles in Greek history. King George I chose this as the text for a national anthem, which the composer Nikolaos Manzaros (1795-1873) subsequently set to music. In 1864 King Otto requested musical authorities in Bavaria to evaluate the merit of Manzaros' work. Since no negative opinions were cited, the music and text became the official national anthem in that year. Only the first two verses are performed as the national anthem.

GRENADA
Hail! Grenada, Land Of Ours

Before the country obtained independence, Grenada was under British sovereignty. The anthem composed by Louis Masanto Jr., with text by Irva Baptista, was officially adopted on Independence Day, February 7, 1974, and replaced *God Save The Queen*.

GUATEMALA
¡Guatemala feliz!

In 1887, on the 50th anniversary of its independence from Spain, Guatemala held a national competition to select a national anthem. The winning composition was by José Joaquín Palma (1844-1911) and Rafael Álvarez (1858-1948).

HAITI
La Dessalinienne

Written in 1903 to commemorate the centennial of independence from French rule, *La Dessalinienne* is named after Jean-Jacques Dessalines, the man credited with the defeat of the French in 1803. It is sung in French, the official language of Haiti.

Another unofficial anthem, *Quand nos aieux briserent leurs entraves*, was used as the national anthem for ten years prior to the adoption of *La Dessalinienne*. Like Costa Rica, Haiti did not have an anthem until the arrival of visitors from another country deemed it necessary. In 1893 a German man-of-war anchored off the coast of Port-au-Prince. A reception was scheduled on board the ship, and the German hosts planned to perform the Haitian national anthem as a part of a ceremony honoring its hosts. The government of Haiti was too embarrassed to admit that there was no anthem. A prominent musician, Occide Jeanty, quickly composed a melody to the words of the patriotic poem by Oswald Durand. Today this song is still used as a presidential song.

HONDURAS
Tu bandera, tu bandera un lampo de cielo

Composer Carlos Hartling (1875-1919) was a prominent musician and patriotic citizen of his country. He established the first symphony orchestra in Central America and helped permanently station military bands in the larger cities. Augusto Constancio Coello (1881-1941) wrote the text. This anthem was chosen as a result of a public competition and adopted in 1915.

IRISH REPUBLIC
Amhrán na bhFiann

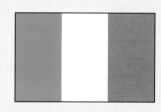

Amhrán na bhFiann (Soldiers Are We) was written by Peadar Kearney (1883-1942) in collaboration with Patrick Heeney (d1911). Known as "The Soldier Song," it was first printed in a 1912 edition of *Irish Freedom*, a monthly publication expressing the views of the Irish Republican Brotherhood. The song was adopted as the national anthem of *Éire* (the Republic of Ireland) in 1926. Although Ireland at that time was still a Dominion of England, it was progressing towards becoming an independent republic, which was finally achieved in 1949.

ISRAEL
Hatiqvah

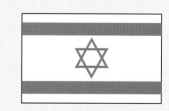

This piece serves not only as the national anthem for the State of Israel, but also functions to unite Jewish people throughout the world. The text is the poem *Hatiqvah*, which was written about 1878 by Naftali Herz Imber (1856-1909). In 1886 it was published in Jerusalem. Two years later Samuel Cohen adapted the melody of a Moldavian folksong arranged by G. Popovici to fit *Hatiqvah*.

ITALY
Inno di Mameli

Fratelli d'Italia (Brothers Of Italy) was written by the patriot and poet Goffredo Mameli (1827-1849) who was killed in battle defending the newly formed Roman Republic in 1849. The text was set to music by Michele Novaro (1822-1885) in 1847. Novaro's fiery song is now usually referred to as *Inno di Mameli* (Mameli's Hymn) as both a tribute to the martyred patriot and a reminder of the long struggle for Italian unification that cut his life short. In 1946 *Inno di Mameli* became the first official national anthem of Italy.

JAMAICA
Eternal Father, Bless Our Land

Prior to its current standing as a member of The Commonwealth of Nations with Dominion Status, Jamaica was ruled by Britain. On August 6, 1962 the country gained its independence and adopted the new national anthem. The music was composed by Robert Lightbourne and the words are by Hugh Sherlock (b.1905).

JAPAN
Kimigayo

Kimigayo (The Reign Of Our Emperor) uses an anonymous text taken from the seventh volume of *Kokinshu* which dates back to the 9th Century. This lyrical text uses poetic metaphor to wish the Emperor longevity. In 1860 Englishman John William Fenton, the first bandmaster of the Japanese Army, set *Kimigayo* to music. In 1880 Hiromori Hayashi, a musician in the Imperial Court, composed music written for traditional Japanese instruments. This arrangement was premiered on November 3, 1880, for the birthday of Emperor Meiji. It was adapted to a Western musical scale by the German successor to Benton, Franz Eckert. *Kimigayo* was officially adopted in 1888.

LATVIA
Dievs Seveti Latviju

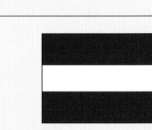

Karlis Baumanis entered this anthem in a competition held during the First Latvian Song Festival in 1873. Although still under czarist Russian rule, the music was composed as a national anthem for an independent Latvian state. This did not occur until November 18, 1918. Twenty-two years later Latvia was again overtaken, this time by the Soviet government. It was not until August of 1991 that the country regained independence. In September of that same year they were admitted to the United Nations.

Traditionally a choir leads the singing of the anthem.

LIBERIA
All Hail, Liberia, Hail!

Liberia (Land Of Freedom) was founded in 1822 by emancipated North American slaves. They established the capital city of Monrovia, named after the American president James Monroe. Composed in 1860 by Olmstead Luca (b.1836), the text was written by the third president of Liberia, Daniel Basheil Warner (1864-1868).

MEXICO
Mexicanos, al grito de guerra

Los Estados Unidos Mexicanos (The United States of Mexico) adopted *Mexicanos, al grito de guerra* (Mexicans, At The Cry Of War) as its national anthem in 1854. A committee of poets and musicians had been formed to select a proper poem as the text for an anthem. They chose the words of the Mexican poet Francisco González Bocanegra (1824-1861). A competition with a prize of five hundred dollars was offered for the best musical setting of Bocanegra's poem. Music of the Spanish composer Jaime Nunó (1824-1908) was chosen to become the *Himno Nacional Mexicano*.

NEW ZEALAND
God Defend New Zealand

God Save The Queen was the only official national anthem until 1977 when *God Defend New Zealand* was accorded equal status to the British anthem. Thomas Bracken (1843-1898) was born in Ireland but brought up in New Zealand. He wrote the text to *God Defend New Zealand* in 1878. During the same year the *Saturday Advertiser* held a competition for the best musical setting of the text. John Woods, an Australian teaching in New Zealand, had the winning entry; the new piece became a favorite patriotic song.

NICARAGUA
Salve a tí Nicaragua

The melody of this anthem has been sung since the early days of its independence, although the composer is unknown. The original text was replaced in 1939 due to its mediocrity. The new text by Salomón Ibarra Mayorga poetically surpasses its predecessor.

The song *Hermosa sorberana* (music by A. Cousin and words by Blas Villatas) is another favored patriotic song sometimes considered a national anthem.

NORTH KOREA (KOREAN DEMOCRATIC PEOPLE'S REPUBLIC)
Ach'im ûn pinnara

After World War II Russian troops occupied Korea. In 1947, shortly before *Chosun Minchu-chui Inmin Koughwa-guk* (The Korean Democratic People's Republic) was officially established in the northern peninsula, *Ach'im ûn pinnara* was adopted as its national anthem.

NORWAY
Ja, vi elsker

Ja, vi elsker (Yes, We Love With Fond Devotion) became the national anthem of the *Kongeriket Norge* (Kingdom of Norway) on May 17, 1864, the fiftieth anniversary of the adoption of the Norwegian constitution. The Nobel Prize winning author of the poem, Bjørnstjerne Bjørnson (1832-1910), later commented on his lyrics: "Our national anthem is that of a small, peace-loving nation, but if it is sung in the hour of danger, determination clad in armour speaks from every line."

Sonner af Norge det aeldgamle rige is also considered a national anthem. The music was composed by Christian Blom (1782-1861), a director of an insurance company. Both works have the status of national anthem.

PANAMA
Himno Istmeño

Jorge Santos emigrated from Spain in 1889 and established himself in Panama City. He wrote the music for *Himno Istmeño* to a text by Juan Agustin Torres. A new text by Jerónimo de la Ossa was written and first performed on November 4, 1903 (the day after Independence Day) as the people of Panama carried their new flag through the streets of their capital. The *Himno Istmeño* was not officially adopted until 1925.

PARAGUAY
A los pueblos

There is some dispute about the actual composer of *A los pueblos*. Although Francés Dupuy or Louis Cavedagni are traditionally credited with the composition, there is evidence that the music was actually composed by Francisco Esteban Acuña de Figueroa, the author of the text. He also wrote the words to the national anthem of Uruguay. An arrangement of the music by Remberto Gimenéz was declared the official version in May of 1934.

PERU
¡Somos Libres!

José Bernardo Alcedo (1788-1878) was considered a musical innovator in Peru, having published the first Peruvian theory of music entitled *Filosofia Elemental de Musica*. In 1821 he composed the song *¡Somos libres!* (We Are Free!) which was ultimately chosen as the winning composition in a government sponsored competition held to find a national anthem. Its premiere performance was in September of 1821 in the Teatro Segura of Lima. A revision of the original work was made by Claudio Rebagliati in 1869, and that version was declared unalterable by the 1924 Peruvian Congress.

PHILIPPINES
Bayang Magiliw

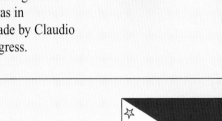

Bayang Magiliw (Land Of The Morning) grew out of the 1898 Philippine revolution against Spain. In 1898 General Emilio Aquinaldo, leader of the Philippine revolution, requested Julian Felipe (1861-1944) to compose a patriotic march only a few days before independence was declared. The result was the *Bayang Magiliw* which was premiered on June 12, 1898 at the reading of the Act of Proclamation of Philippine Independence. This independence only lasted a few months. In December of 1898 Spain sold the Philippines to the United States for twenty million dollars. The Philippines then continued their struggle for independence against the United States. José Palma (1876-1903) added Spanish lyrics to the march in 1899. Philippine independence was finally granted on July 4, 1946. Lyrics in the native Tagalog language finally replaced the Spanish lyrics in 1956.

POLAND
Jeszcze Polska nie zginęla

Jeszcze Polska nie zginęla (Poland Will Not Be Lost) was written in 1797 by Józef Wybicki (1747-1822) while the Polish Legion was stationed in Italy. An argument can be made that the music was composed by Michal Kleofas Oginski (1765-1833). The piece was the marching song of the unit led by General J.H. Dabrowski, and therefore was given the name *Mazurek Dabrowskiego* (Dabrowski Mazurka). During the nineteenth century the piece remained popular as a patriotic song. It was officially adopted as the Polish National Anthem in 1926.

RUSSIA
from A Life For The Czar

Glinka has long been considered one of Russia's most nationalistic composers. When Russia became an independent state on December 26, 1991 as a result of the dissolution of the Soviet Union, music taken from his opera *A Life For The Czar* replaced the Soviet anthem. There is no text. This choice reflects the tide of nationalism currently found in Russia.

SLOVAKIA
Nad Tatrou Sa Blyska

Poet Janko Matúska (1821-1877) wrote the words for *Nad Tatrou Sa Blyska* (Over The Tatra Mountains) in 1844. The melody is an old Slovakian folksong which told of the exodus of Slovak students from Bratislava in 1843. During the years that the Czech and Slovak nations were united as a federation, the anthems were performed concurrently. On January 1, 1993 the federation was dissolved and the national anthems became independent. Traditionally a symphony orchestra leads the audience in singing.

SOUTH AFRICA
Die Stem van Suid-Afrika

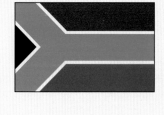

Die Stem van Suid-Afrika was composed by C.J. Langehoven (1873-1932). A better poet than composer, a search was begun immediately to find a more appropriate melody. The Cape newspaper *Die Burger* held the competition and music by Rev. Marthinus Lourens de Villiers (1885-1977) was declared the winner. The premiere was held on May 31, 1928 with Rev. de Villiers conducting a mass choir of school children. *Die Stem van Suid-Afrika* was officially adopted as the South African national anthem in 1936. A competition held to find the best English translation attracted two-hundred twenty entries. In 1952 during the celebrations marking the tercentenary of the Dutch settlement of the Cape of Good Hope the South African national anthem was sung for the first time in English using the winning translation, "Ringing out from our blue heavens..."

SOUTH KOREA (KOREAN REPUBLIC)
Tonghai moolkwa Paiktusani

The words of the national anthem of *Taehan Min'guk* (The Republic of Korea) were written toward the end of the nineteenth century either by Yun Ch'i-ho (1865-1946) or An Ch'ang-ho (1878-1938). The poem is still known as *Aegukka* (A Song Of Love Of Country). At that time it was sung to the melody of Robert Burn's *Auld Lang Syne*. From 1910-1945, the period of Japanese colonial rule, the song was banned in Korea. In 1935 Eak Tay Ahn (1906-1965), a Korean living in Spain, composed a new melody for *Aegukka*. This setting was sung at a ceremony celebrating the founding of the Republic on August 15, 1948.

SPAIN
Marcha real

One of the oldest national anthems in use today, King Carlos decreed *Marcha real* as the Spanish royal march on September 3, 1770. One hundred years later King Amadeo I decided to hold a competition for a new anthem. Although over four hundred songs were entered, none of them was chosen to replace *Marcha real*. A military band usually performs the anthem, although it may also be performed by an orchestra. The music is anonymous and there is no text.

SWEDEN
Du gamla, du fria

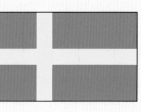

The text to *Du gamla, du fria* (Thou Ancient, Thou Freeborn) was written by Richard Dybeck (1811-1877) in 1844 using a folk melody he heard in the province of Västmanland. Other patriotic songs were introduced in Sweden about this time which vied for popularity with *Du gamla, du fria*, but sometime between 1880-1890 Dybeck's song came to be generally regarded as the national anthem of the *Konungariket Sverige* (Kingdom of Sweden).

SWITZERLAND
Swiss Psalm

Prior to 1961 Switzerland had no official national anthem, although *Rufst du, mein Vaterland?,* sung to the tune of *God Save The Queen,* functioned as one. In 1841 Alberik Zwyssig (1808-1854) replaced the words to his religious hymn *Diligam te, Domine* with the text by Leonhard Widmer (1808-1867). *Trittst im Morgenrot daher* (On Your Mountains) had its premiere in 1843 at a Zurich singing festival. It was not until 1961 that it was adopted on trial for three years as the national anthem. The decision was postponed at the end of the three years. Being a multi-lingual country, the anthem is always presented in German, French, Italian, Surselvisch and Ladinisch.

UGANDA
Pearl Of Africa

Until 1962 Uganda was under the protection of Great Britain. On October 9 of that year the country declared its independence. The music composed by George Kakoma was the winning entry in the competition to select a new national anthem. Affiliated with the Music Department of Makerere College in Kampala, Uganda, he collaborated on the lyrics with Peter Wyngard, a colleague from the English Department. The premiere was broadcast in August of 1962 on all radio stations in Uganda.

UKRAINE
Shche ne vmerla Ukrania

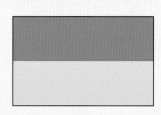

Paul Chubïnsky (1839-1884) and Mikhail Verbïtsky (1815-1870) wrote *Shche ne vmerla Ukrania* (Ukraine Lives On) in 1863. Verbïtsky was inspired by Chubïnsky's patriotic poem and resolved to turn it into a national anthem. In 1864 it was performed as a choral work at the Ukraine Theatre in L'vov. It was adopted as the Ukrainian national anthem during the revolution of 1917. Ukrainians were forbidden to perform *Shche ne vmerla Ukrania* during the reign of the Soviet regime. Upon becoming a republic in 1990 the Ukrainian government officially reinstated *Shche ne vmerla Ukrania* as its national anthem.

UNITED STATES OF AMERICA
The Star-Spangled Banner

The darkest days of America's second war with England came in August of 1814, when British troops marched on Washington, D.C. and burned down both the Capitol and the White House. By September their sights were set on Fort McHenry in Baltimore. An elderly civilian citizen, Dr. William Beanes, was mistakenly taken prisoner during the British army's approach to the city. Francis Scott Key (1779-1843), a lawyer from Georgetown and a friend of Dr. Beanes, went to meet the Admiral of the British fleet in order to secure the release of his friend. Key won his friend's release but, with the bombardment of Fort McHenry about to begin, both men were detained aboard a British ship during the night of September 13.

As Key watched the bombardment of Fort McHenry from the ship's deck, he jotted down some ideas for the first stanza of *The Star-Spangled Banner* on the back of an envelope. He added three more stanzas the next day and named his poem *Defence of Fort McHenry*. Key quickly had his poem printed and posted throughout Baltimore while the citizens celebrated the withdrawal of British forces. Someone suggested singing the poem to the tune of John Stafford Smith's *To Anachreon In Heaven*. Within a month the song and text were united. Key renamed his song *The Star-Spangled Banner*.

To Anachreon In Heaven became popular in the United States after the Revolutionary War. It was composed in 1770 for the London Anacreontic Society, an aristocratic group dedicated to the promotion of the arts, by John Stafford Smith (1750-1836). When war erupted with the British in 1812, Smith's tune was well enough known to be used for several patriotic parodies such as *Adams And Liberty* and *The Boston Patriotic Song*.

On March 3, 1931 an Act of Congress officially designated *The Star-Spangled Banner* as the United States' national anthem.

URUGUAY
¡Orientales, la patria o la tumba!

A government decree established this national anthem in 1845. The music was composed by Fernando Quijano (1805-1871) and Franciso José Deballi (1793-1859). Deballi was a native Hungarian who immigrated to Uruguay in 1838. Francisco Esteban Acuña de Figueroa (1791-1862), in addition to writing the text to this anthem, authored the text to the national anthem of Paraguay.

VENEZUELA
Gloria al bravo pueblo

Gloria al bravo pueblo (Glory To The Nation) was written during the earliest attempts of the country to gain its independence from Spain. Both the composer Juan José Landaeta (1780-1814) and lyricist Vincente Salias were executed in 1814 for their role in the revolution. Finally in 1821 Venezuela won its independence. *Gloria al bravo pueblo* is the oldest of the Latin-American anthems, and gained official status as national anthem on May 25, 1881. Traditional performance is done in one of the following ways: military band, a capella choir, orchestra or occasionally a solo singer.

VIETNAM
Tiên quân ca

In July of 1976, the first session of the newly appointed United National Assembly declared *Tiên quân ca* as the anthem for the entire country. This was the anthem of the former North Vietnam which was first adopted in 1946. The South Vietnamese anthem was penned by a student, Luu Huu Phouc. *Thanh Nien Hanh Khuc* was the anthem used in South Vietnam from 1948-1976.

THE ANTHEMS

AUSTRALIA
Advance Australia Fair

Words and Music by
PETER DODDS McCORMICK

Majestically

AUSTRIA
Land der Berge, Land am Strome

Words by PAULA von PRERADOVIĆ
Music by JOHANN HOLZER

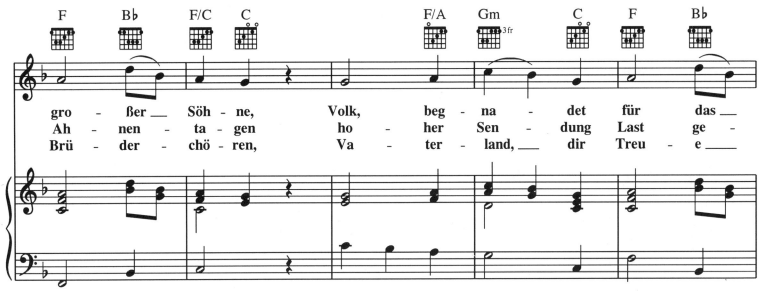

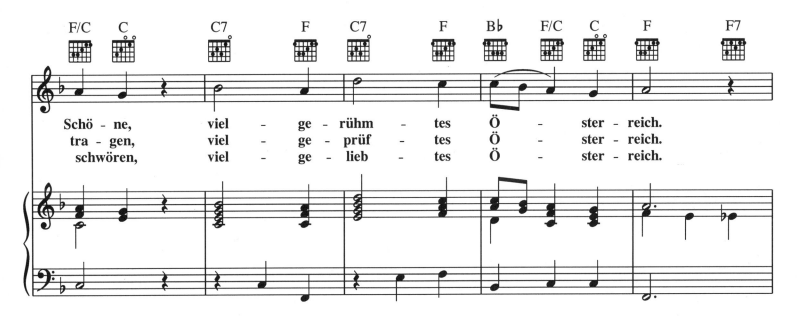

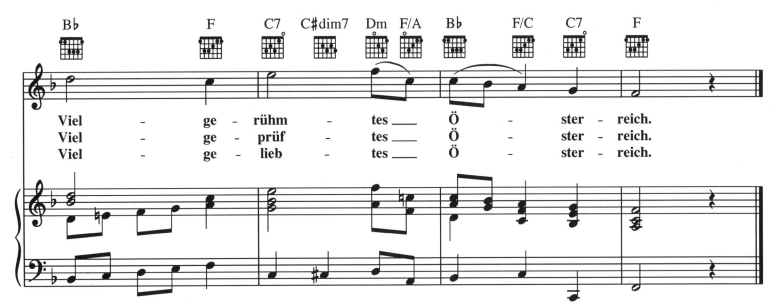

English Translation

1. Land of mountains, land of rivers,
   Land of tillage, land of churches,
   Land of iron, land of promise.
   Motherland of valiant sons,
   People blessed with beauty's grace.
   Austria of fair renown.

2. Place of feuds and bitter strife,
   At the very heart of Europe;
   Heart that beats with courage high,
   You have borne since times ancestral
   Burdens of a noble mission,
   Austria, sorely tried and tested.

3. See towards the new age dawning,
   Firm in faith and free we march,
   With joy in work and hopeful hearts.
   To thee, oh fatherland united,
   Loyalty we pledge as brothers.
   Austria, our much beloved.

BAHAMAS
March On, Bahamaland!

Words and Music by
TIMOTHY GIBSON

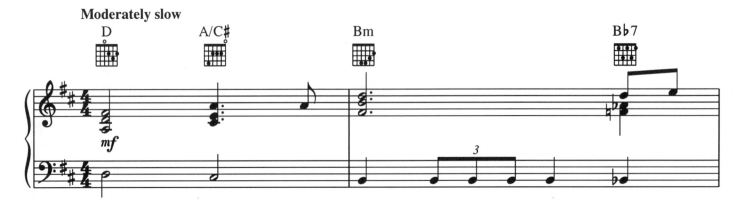

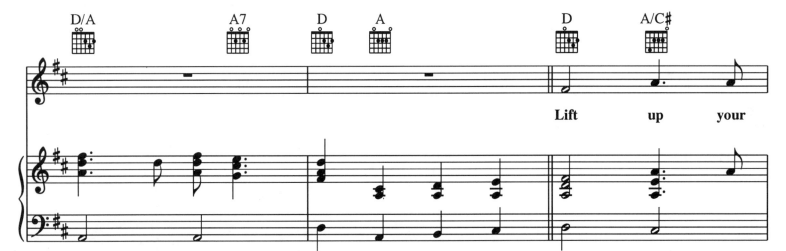

Lift up your

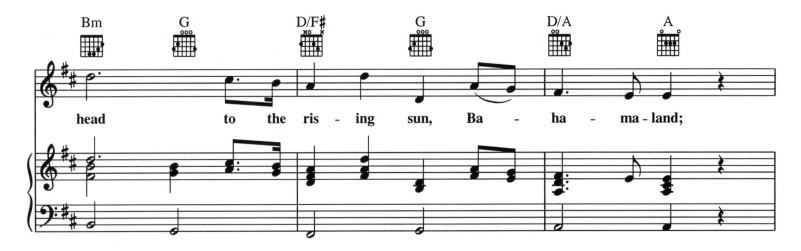

head to the ris - ing sun, Ba - ha - ma - land;

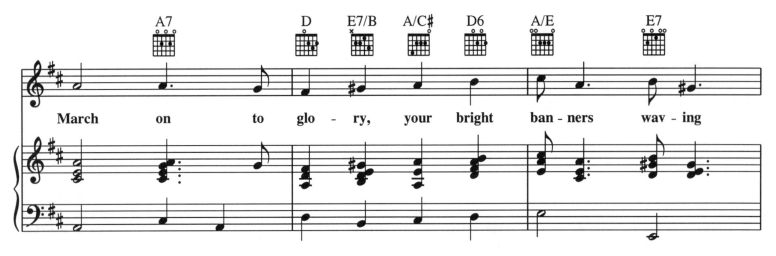

March on to glo - ry, your bright ban - ners wav - ing

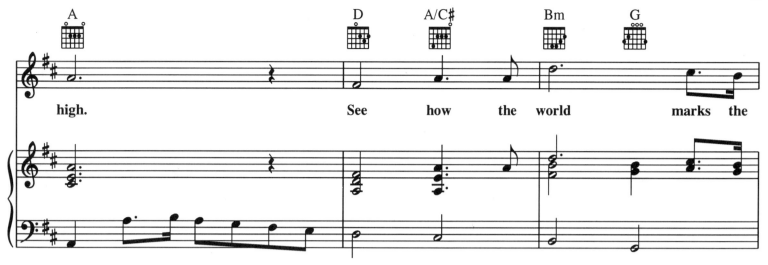

high. See how the world marks the

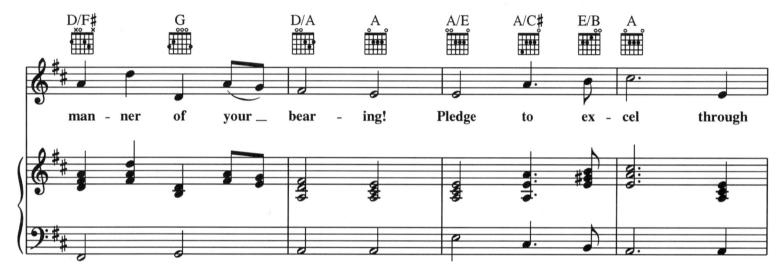

man - ner of your __ bear - ing! Pledge to ex - cel through

love and __ u - ni - ty. Press - ing on - ward, march to -

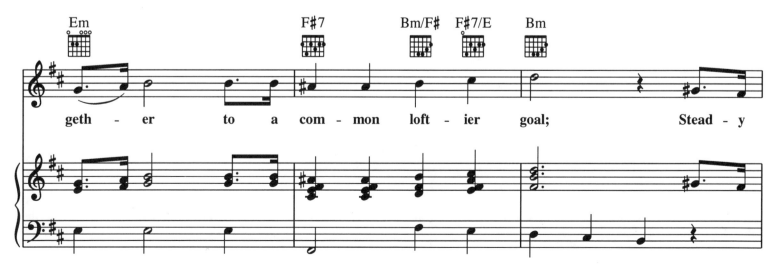

geth - er to a com - mon loft - ier goal; Stead - y

BARBADOS
In Plenty And In Time Of Need

Words by IRVINE LOUIS BURGIE
Music by VAN ROLAND EDWARDS

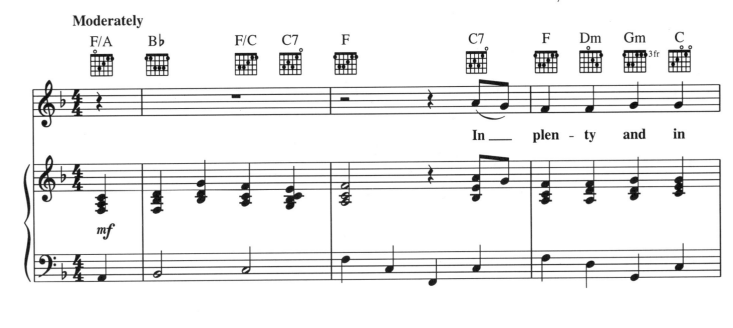

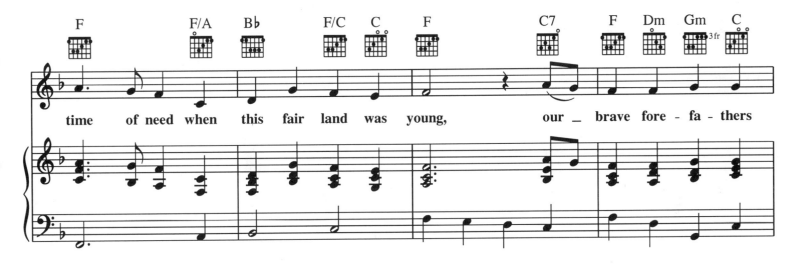

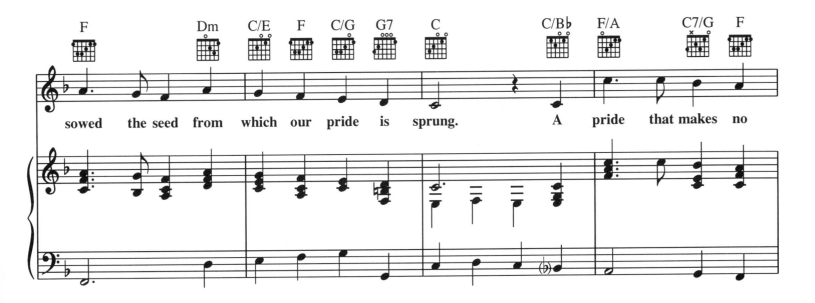

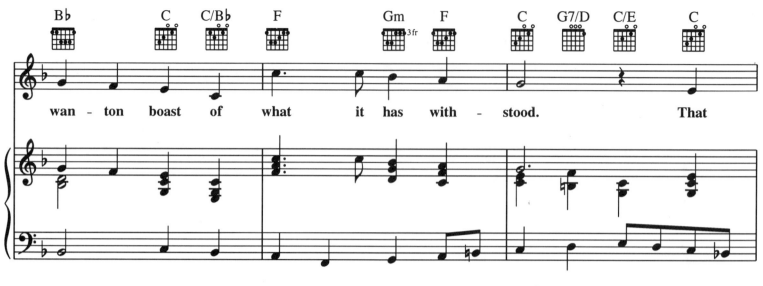

wan - ton boast of what it has with - stood. That

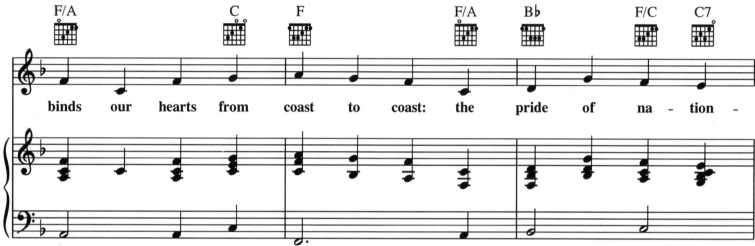

binds our hearts from coast to coast: the pride of na - tion -

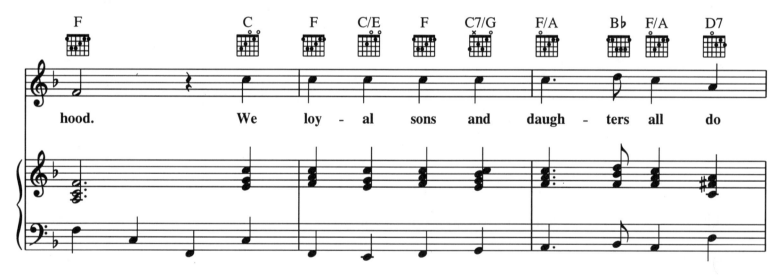

hood. We loy - al sons and daugh - ters all do

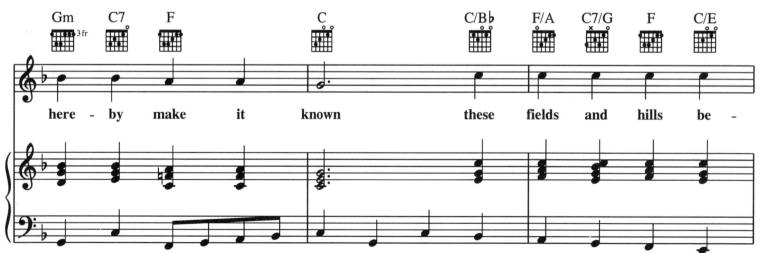

here - by make it known these fields and hills be -

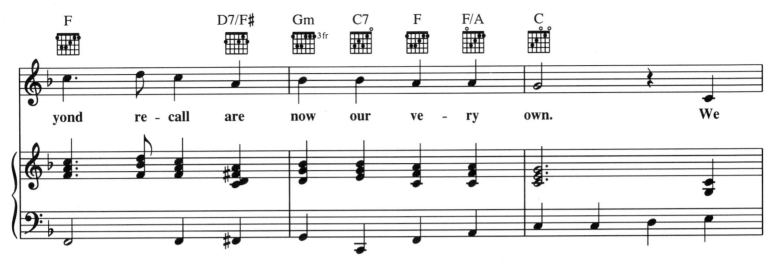

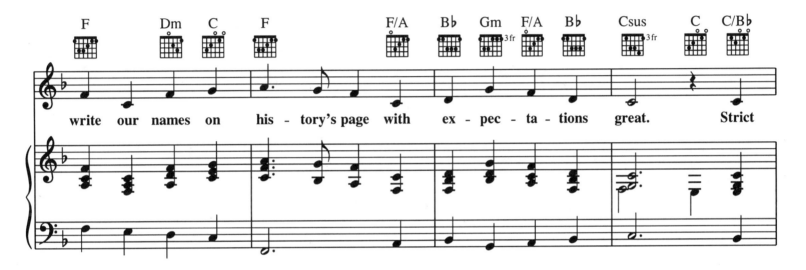

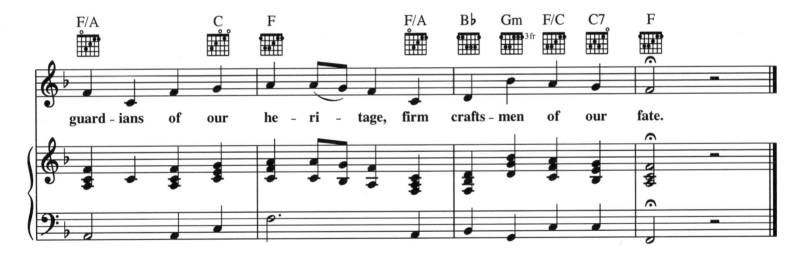

Additional Lyrics

2. The Lord has been the people's guide
   For past three hundred years.
   With Him still on the people's side
   We have no doubts or fears.
   Upward and onward we shall go,
   Inspired, exulting, free,
   And greater will our nation grow
   In strength and unity.

To Chorus

BELIZE
O Land Of The Free

Words by SAMUEL ALFRED HAYNES
Music by SELWYN WALFORD YOUNG

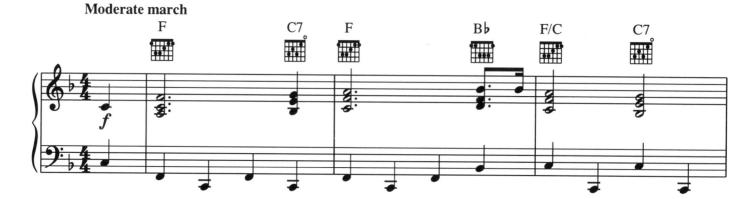

O Land of the Free by the Ca - rib Sea, Our

See additional lyrics

man - hood we pledge to thy li - ber - ty! No ty - rants here lin - ger,

des - pots must flee This tran - quil ha - ven of de - mo - cra - cy. The

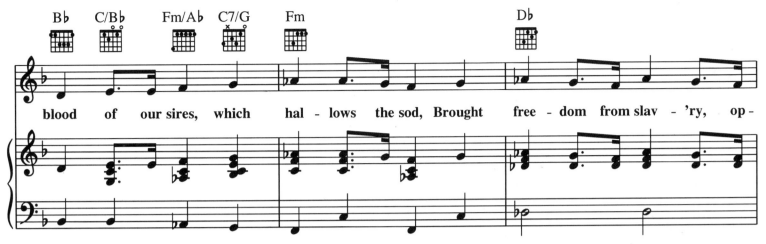

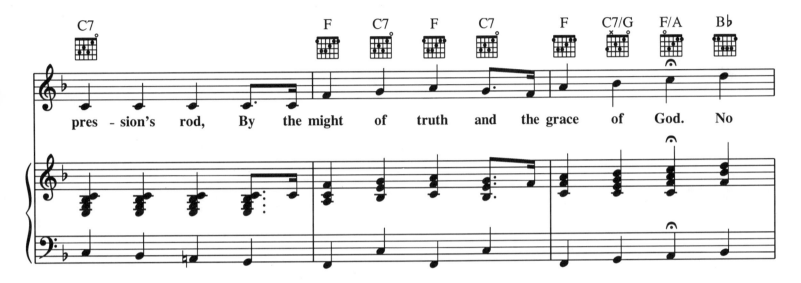

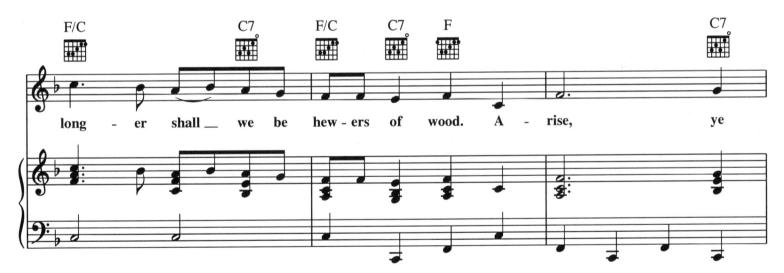

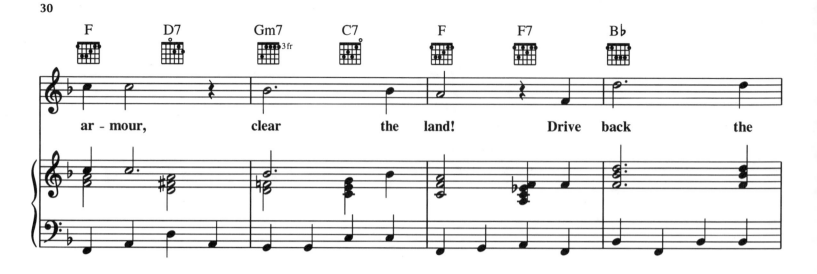

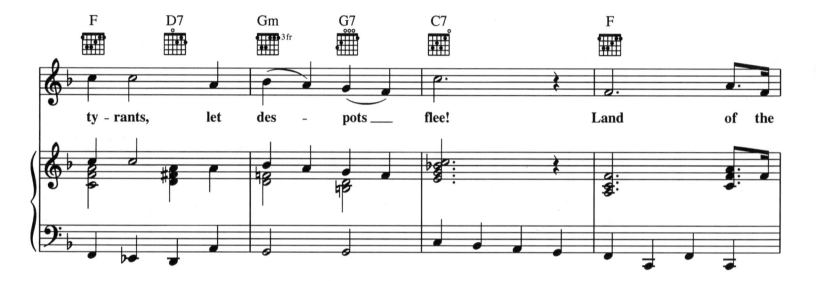

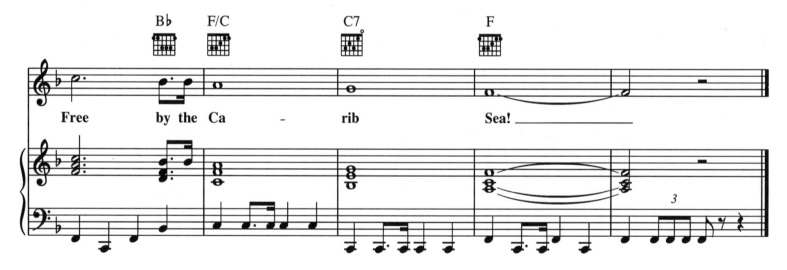

Additional Lyrics

Nature has blessed thee with wealth untold,
O'er mountains and valleys where prairies roll;
Our fathers, the Baymen, valiant and bold
Drove back th'invader, this heritage bold
From proud Rio Hondo to old Sarstoon,
Through coral isle, over blue lagoon,
Keep watch with the angels, the stars and moon.
For freedom comes tomorrow's noon.

Chorus

CHILE
Puro Chile es tu cielo azulado

Words by EUSEBIO LILLO
Music by RAMÓN CARNICER

tien - do en el cam - po de ho - nor.   El que a - yer do - ble - gá - ba se es -

cla - vo   Hoy ya li - bre y triun - fan - te se ve: Hoy ya

li - bre y triun - fan - te ___ se ve: Li - ber -

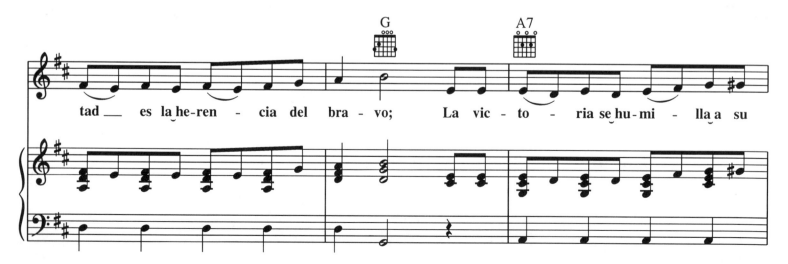

tad ___ es la he - ren - cia del bra - vo;   La vic - to - ria se hu - mi - lla a su

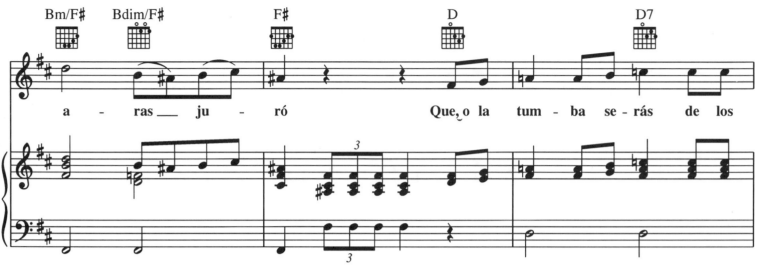

a - ras __ ju - ró   Que, o la tum - ba se - rás de los

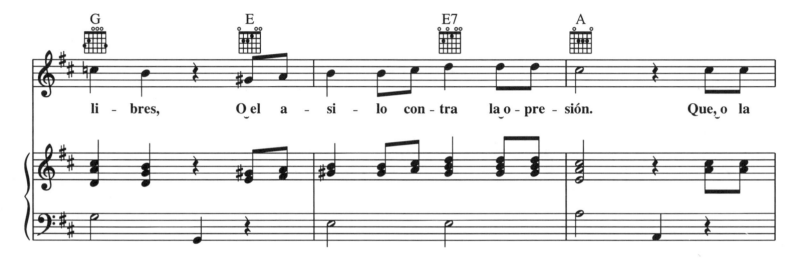

li - bres,   O el a - si - lo con - tra la o - pre - sión.   Que, o la

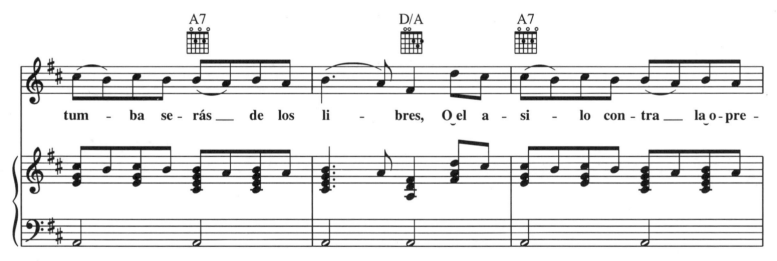

tum - ba se - rás __ de los li - bres,   O el a - si - lo con - tra __ la o - pre -

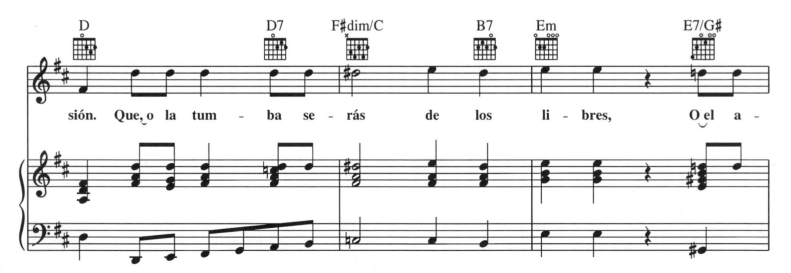

sión. Que, o la tum - ba se - rás   de los   li - bres,   O el a -

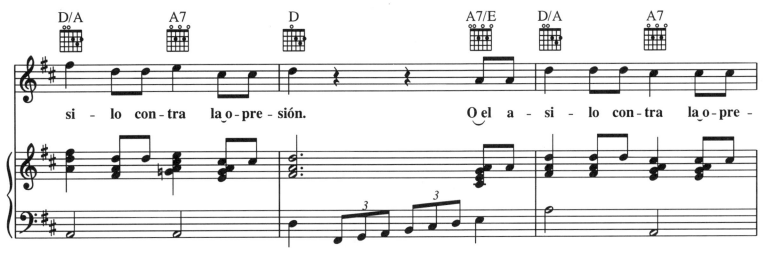

si - lo con-tra la o - pre - sión. O el a - si - lo con-tra la o - pre -

sión. O el a - si - lo con - tra la o - pre - sión.

English Translation

The bloody conflict now is finished
Oppressor and oppressed are now brothers.
The humiliation of the oppressed is surpassed
By the honor gained in battle.

He who yesterday was but a slave in disgrace
Today is free and triumphant,
Today is free and triumphant.

Freedom is the inheritance of the brave,
Victory lies at their feet.
Freedom is the inheritance of the brave,
Victory lies at their feet.

Beautiful Country, receive the vows
That Chileans declared so fervently:
That you should be a shrine of liberty
And a sanctuary against oppression.
That you should be a shrine of liberty
And a sanctuary against oppression.
That you should be a shrine of liberty
And a sanctuary against oppression.
And a sanctuary against oppression.
And a sanctuary against oppression.

BOLIVIA
Bolivianos, el hado propicio

Words by JOSÉ IGNACIO DE SANJINÉS
Music by BENEDETTO VICENTI

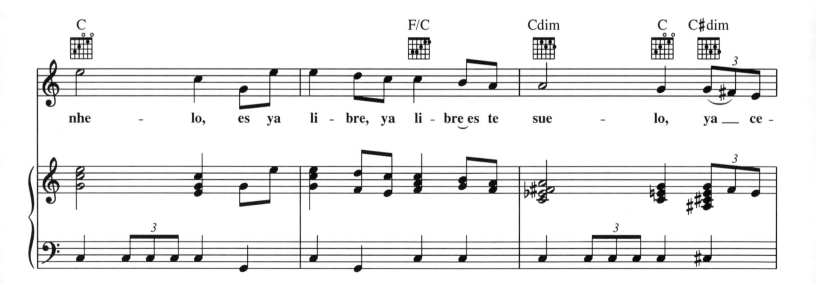

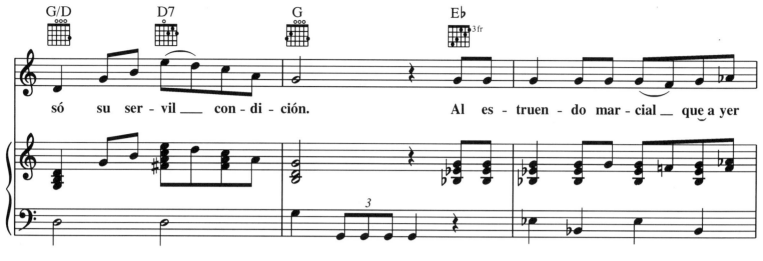

só su ser - vil __ con - di - ción. Al es - truen - do mar - cial __ que a yer

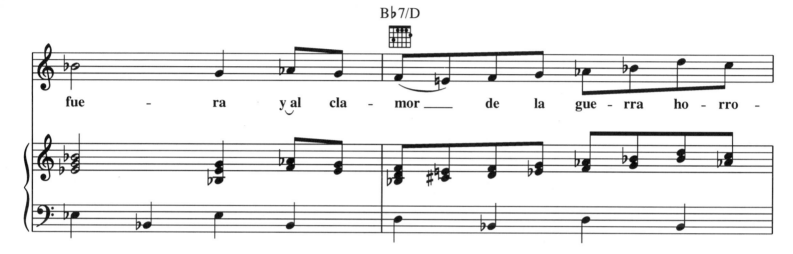

fue _____ ra y al cla - mor ____ de la gue - rra ho - rro -

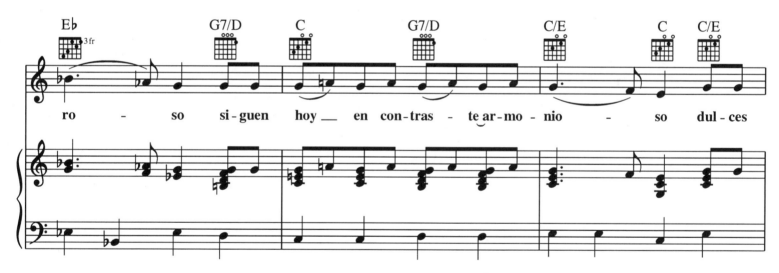

ro _____ so si - guen hoy __ en con - tras - te ar - mo - nio - so dul - ces

him - nos de paz __ y __ de u - nión. Si - guen hoy __ en con - tras - te ar - mo -

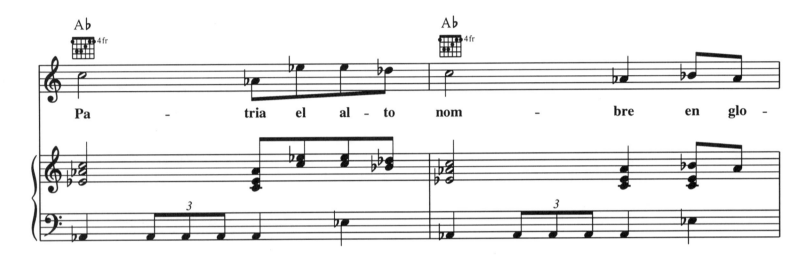

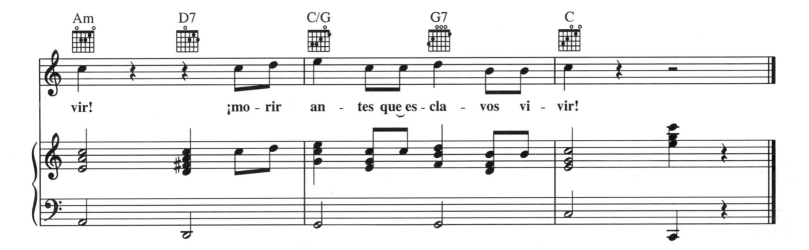

English Translation

Oh, Bolivia, we have been blessed,
And our prayers have been answered.
For now freedom is ours;
The time of servitude is in our past.

Following yesterday's call to duty
And the horrible clamor of war,
Comes today the contrasting harmony
Of sweet hymns of peace and unity;
Comes today the contrasting harmony
Of sweet hymns of peace and unity.

We will defend our country,
The glorious splendor of her name we will maintain.
And we always will proudly proclaim,
"To die is better than a life of slavery!
To die is better than a life of slavery!
To die is better than a life of slavery!"

BRAZIL
Ouviram do Ipirangas as margens placidas

Words by JOAQUIM OSÓRIO DUQUE ESTRADA
Music by FRANCISCO MANOEL DA SILVA

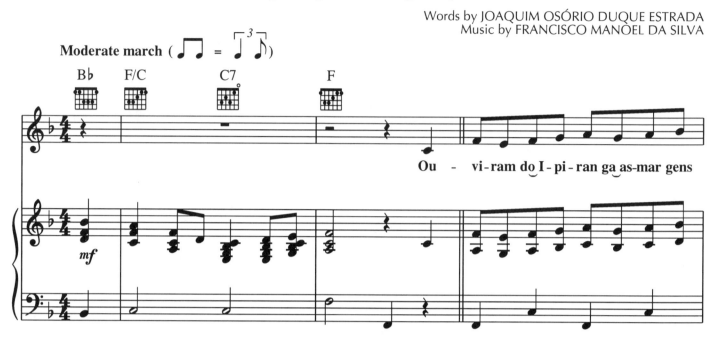

-mor e de es-pe-ran-ça á ter-ra des-ce, Si em teu for-mo-so céo ri-so-nho e

lim - pi-do, Ai - ma-gem do cru-zei-ro res-plan - de - ce. Gi-

-gan - te pe-la pro-pria na-tu-re - za, Es bel-lo és for-te im-pa - vi-do col-

-los - so, E o teu fu-tu-ro es-pe-lha es-sa gran-de za, Ter-ra a-do-

ra - da, en - tre ou - tras mil, Es tu Bra - zil, O! Pa-tria a - ma - da! Dos fi - lhos

des - te so - lo és mãe gen - til, Pa-tria a-ma - da, Bra - zil!

English Translation

The cry rang out from Ipiranga
Called out by the heroic masses.
The sun of liberty cast its rays upon
Those who cherished their nation.

If equality can some day be ours,
We will fight with all our strengthos
Liberty is the precious gift
For which we will gladly die.

Oh, beloved country, we hail you;
Brazil, where the dream of love prevails.
Hope shines upon us like a brilliant ray of sun,
Upon all who live below the sky where glimmers
The magnificence of the Southern Cross.

Comparing you with all others,
You are a fearless giant.
Your future will be determined by your beauty and your strength.

Beloved country, you are loved above all others,
You are mother to us all, beloved country of Brazil.

CANADA
O Canada!

Words by SIR ADOLPHE BASILE ROUTHIER
English version by ROBERT STANLEY WEIR
Music by CALIXA LAVALLÉE

With dignity

O Can - a - da! Our home and na - tive land! True pa - triot
O Can - a - da! Ter - re de nos aï - eux, *Ton front est*

love in all thy sons com - mand. With glow - ing hearts we
ceint de fleur - ons glo - ri - eux! *Car ton bras sait por - ter l'é-*

see thee rise, The True North strong and free! From far and wide, O
pé - e, Il sait por - ter la Croix! *Ton his - toire est une é - po-*

COLOMBIA
¡Oh gloria inmarcesible!

Words by RAFAEL NÚÑEZ
Music by ORESTES SINDICI

¡Oh, gloria in mar ce si - ble! ¡Oh, jú - bi - lo in - mor - tal! En sur - cos de do - lo - res El bien ger - mi - na

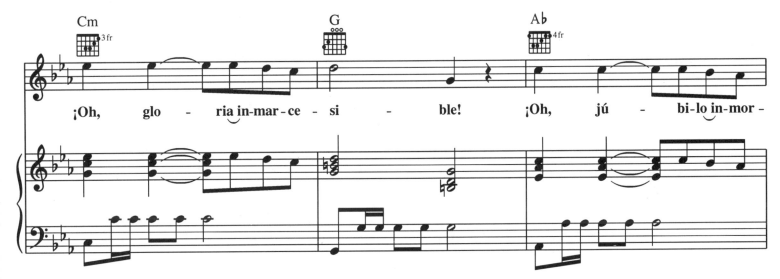

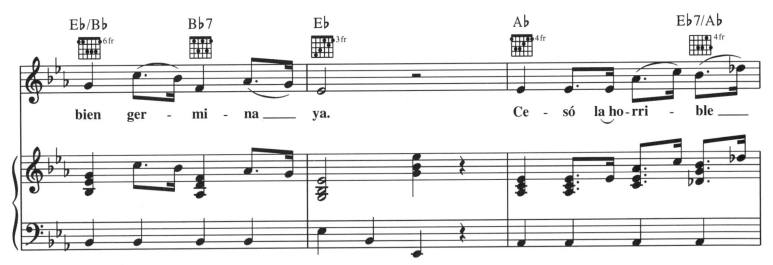

no - che, La li - ber - tad ___ su - bli - me

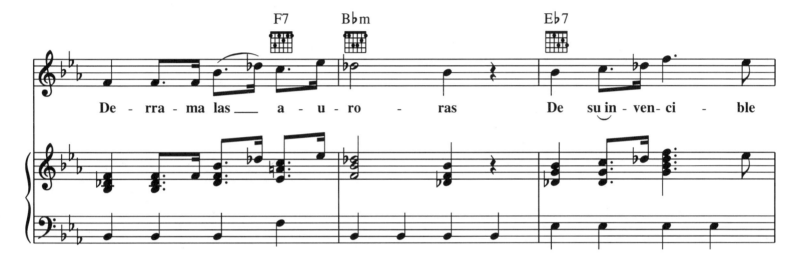

De - rra - ma las ___ a - u - ro - ras De su in - ven - ci - ble

luz. La hu - ma - ni - dad en - te - ra, Que en -

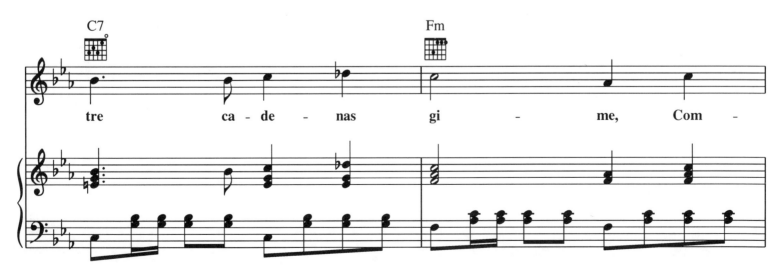

tre ca - de - nas gi - me, Com -

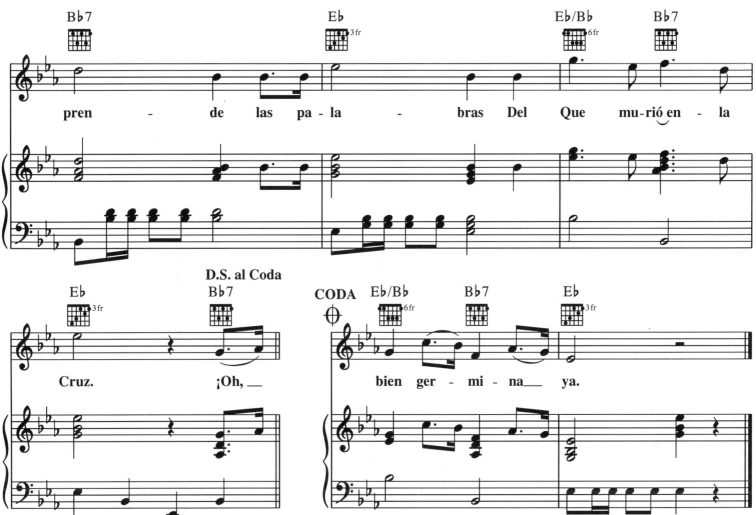

English Translation

Unfading glory! Immortal gladness!
In furrows of sadness
The good has grown,
The horrible night has ended.
Sublime liberty is spilling into the dawn
With invincible light.
All people groaning in chains
Understand the words of He who died on the cross.

COSTA RICA
Noble patria

Words by JOSE MARÍA ZELEDÓN BRENES
Music by MANUEL MARÍA GUTIÉRREZ

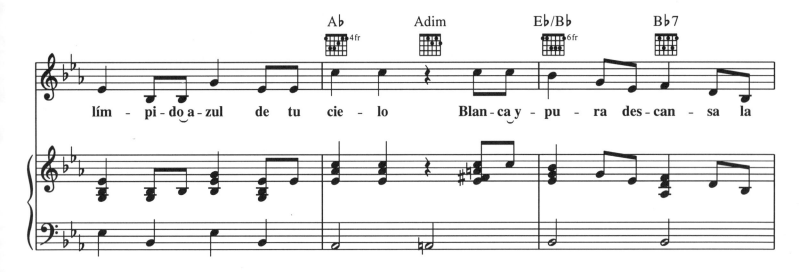

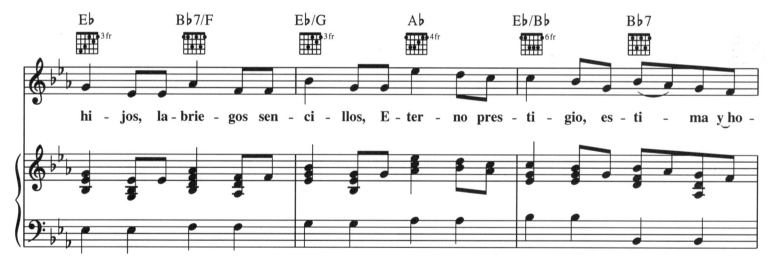

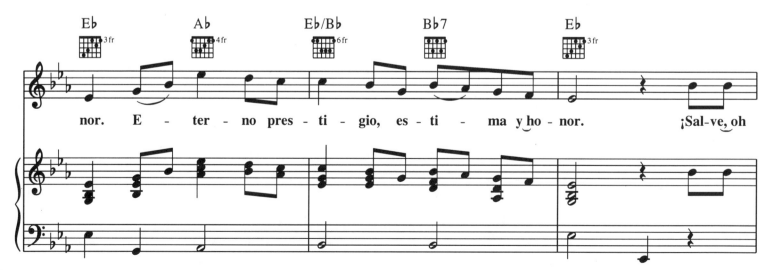

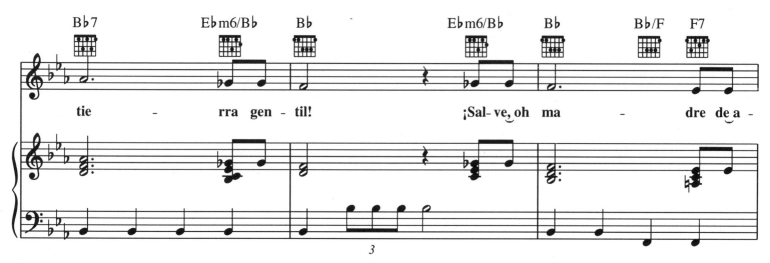

tie - rra gen - til! ¡Sal-ve, oh ma - dre de a -

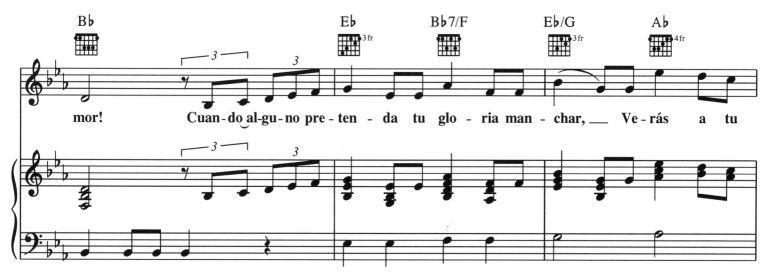

mor! Cuan-do al-gu-no pre-ten - da tu glo-ria man-char, ___ Ve-rás a tu

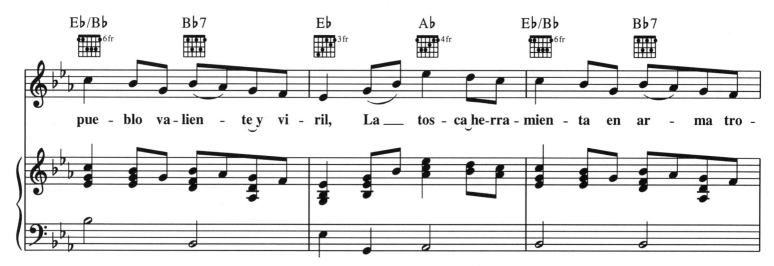

pue - blo va-lien - te y vi-ril, La ___ tos-ca he-rra-mien - ta en ar - ma tro -

car. ¡Sal-ve, oh pa - tria! tu pró - di-go sue-lo Dul-ce a -

English Translation

Noble country, your beautiful flag
Expresses to us the story of your life;
Beneath the clear blue of your sky
Lies the pure whiteness of peace.

The hard-working life below your skies
That has reddened the skin of all men
Has brought great renown to all.
High esteem, prestige, and honor are ours.
High esteem, prestige, and honor are ours.

We extol thee, oh gentle land!
We extol thee, our loving mother!
If intruders should come, we will be called to arms.
Your proud people will leave their homes
And replace the tools of their trade with weapons of war.

We extol thee, oh bounteous country!
You give us ever-increasing happiness.
Beneath the clear blue of your sky
We will forever work and live in peace!

CUBA
La bayamesa

Words and Music by
PEDRO FIGUEREDO

Triumphantly

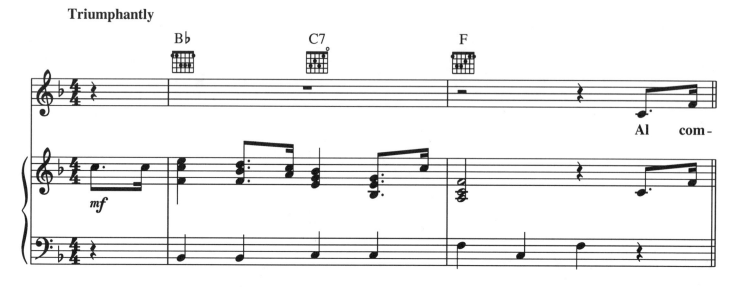

Al com-

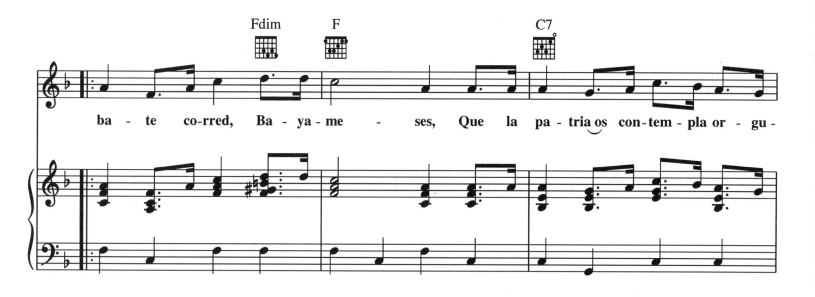

ba - te co-rred, Ba - ya - me - ses, Que la pa - tria os con-tem - pla or - gu-

llo - sa; No te - máis u - na muer - te glo - rio - sa, Que mo-

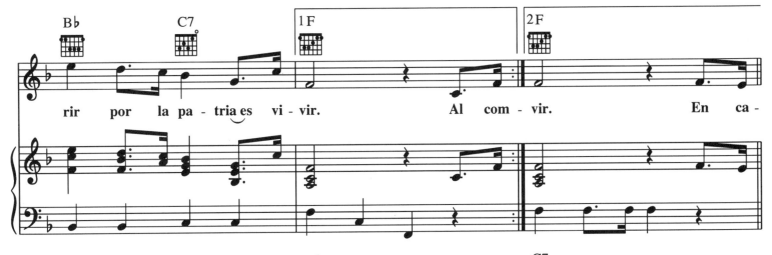

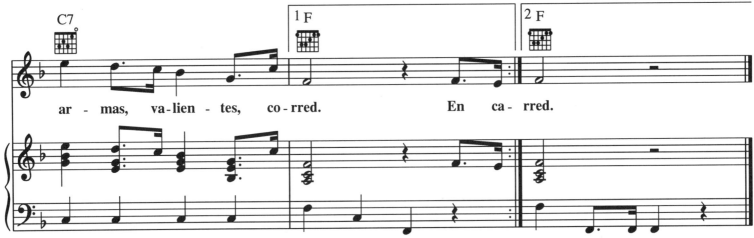

English Translation

Run to the battle, Bayameses.
Proudly regard the country.
Don't fear a glorious death.
To die for the country is to live!

To live in chains is to die!
In disgrace and dishonor surrounded,
The trumpet will sound.
Run to rise to arms!

CZECH REPUBLIC
Kde Domov Můj?

Words by JOSEF KAJETÁN TYL
Music by FRANTIŠEK JAN ŠKROUP

English Translation

Where is my home, where is my home?
Waters murmur through the meadow,
The woods rustle all over the rocky hills,
The spring blossom opens in the orchard,
Oh, to look at this earthly paradise!
And what a beautiful country,
The Czech land, my home,
The Czech land, my home!

DOMINICAN REPUBLIC
Quisqueyanos valientes, alcemos

Words by EMILIO PRUD'HOMME
Music by JOSÉ REYÉS

dón. ¡Sal - ve el-pue - blo que, in-tré - pi - do y fuer - te, A la

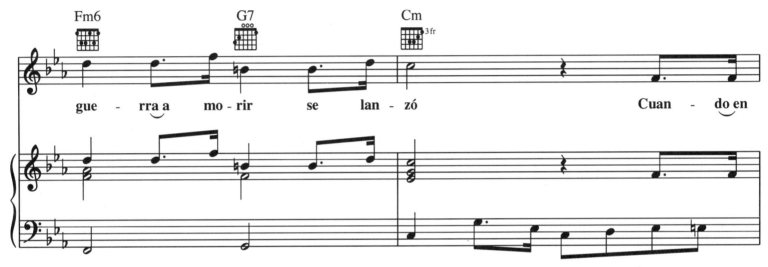

gue - rra a mo - rir se lan - zó Cuan - do en

bé - li - co re - to de muer - te Sus ca - de - nas de es - cla - vo rom-

no chord

pió.

Nin - gun pue - blo ser li - bre me -

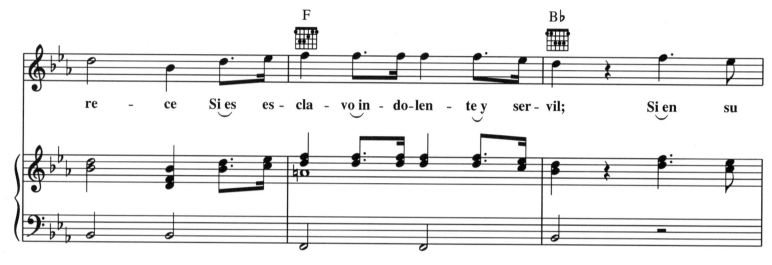

re - ce Si es es - cla - vo in - do - len - te y ser - vil; Si en su

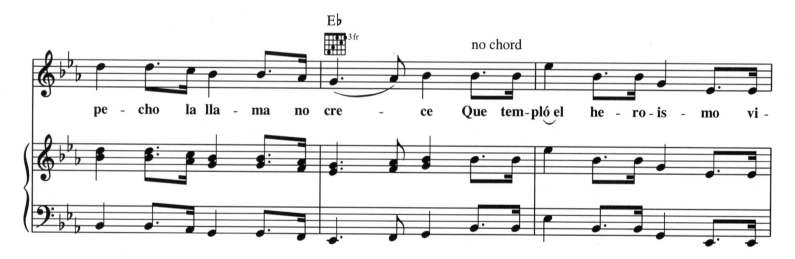

pe - cho la lla - ma no cre - ce Que tem - pló el he - ro - is - mo vi -

ril. Mas_ Quis - que - ya la in - dó - mi - ta y bra - va Siem - pre al -

English Translation

Valiant Quisqueyanos, we raise our voices in song with heartfelt emotion
And show the world our proud faces and glorious flag.
Hail our brave and strong nation! We would die for our country in war.
The slave's chains have been broken.
No country deserves freedom where slavery and indolence exist.
The cry of freedom must ring out and heroism will win.
Brave and indomitable Santo Domingo, always hold your head up high.
If you were enslaved a thousand times,
You would a thousand times regain your freedom.

ECUADOR
¡Salve, oh patria, mil veces!

Words by JOSE LEÓN MERA
Music by ANTONIO NEUMANE

March

frente, __ tu fren - te ra - dio - sa Más que el sol con - tem - pla - mos lu -

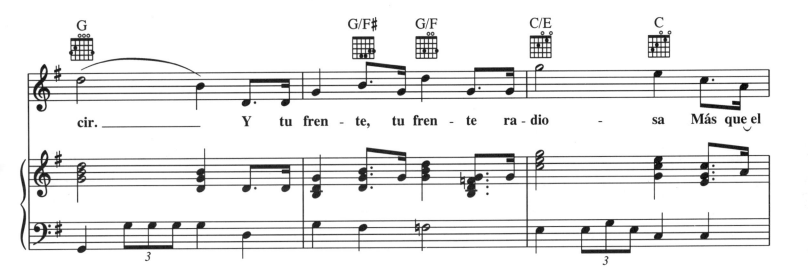

cir. _____ Y tu fren - te, tu fren - te ra - dio - sa Más que el

sol con - tem - pla - mos lu - cir. Y tu cir.

English Translation

May thy freedom be guarded, dear country,
Hail to thee! Hail to thee!
In thy heart there is peace overflowing,
In thy heart, joy and peace overflowing;
And thy face, with its radiance glowing,
Shines much brighter than sunlight appears;
And thy face, with its radiance glowing,
Shines much brighter than sunlight appears.

EL SALVADOR
Saludemos la patria orgullosos

Words by GEN. JUAN J. CAÑAS
Music by JUAN ALBERLE

Moderately

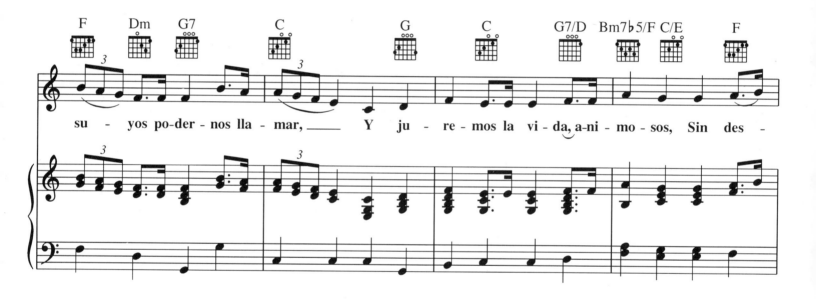

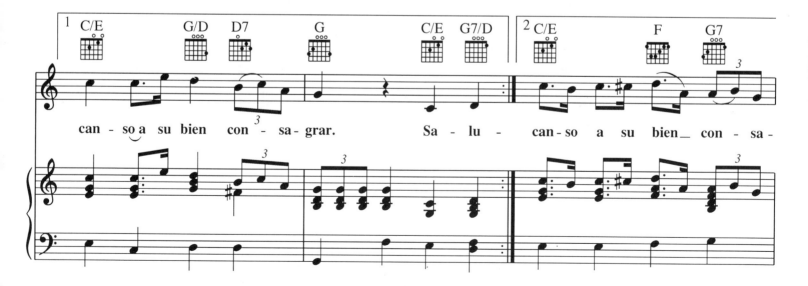

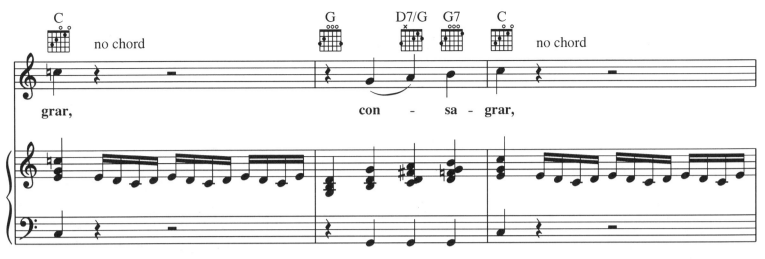

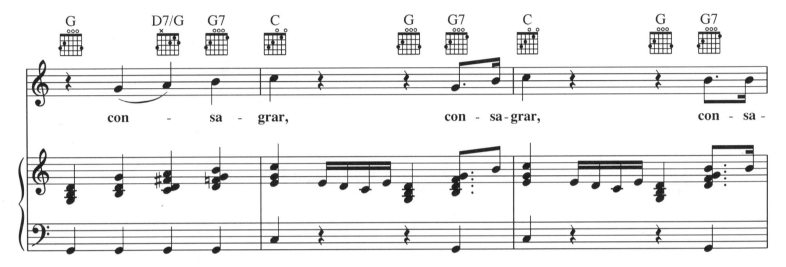

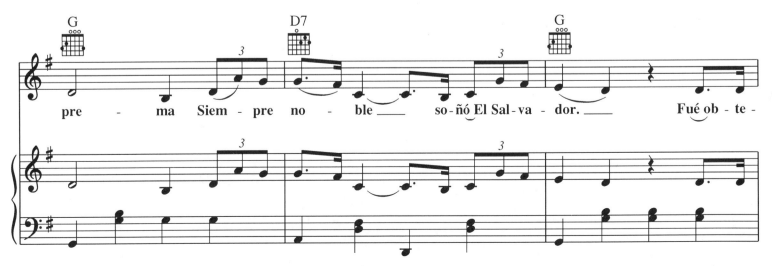

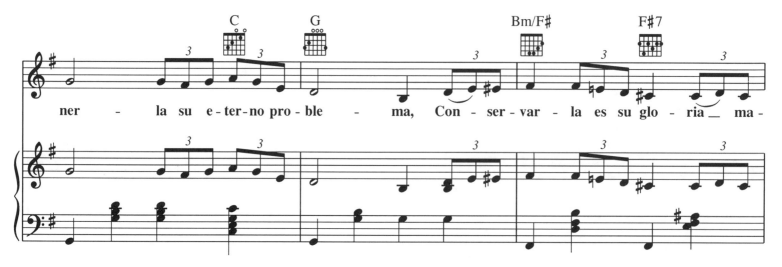

ner - la su e-ter-no pro-ble - ma, Con - ser - var-la es su glo - ria __ ma-

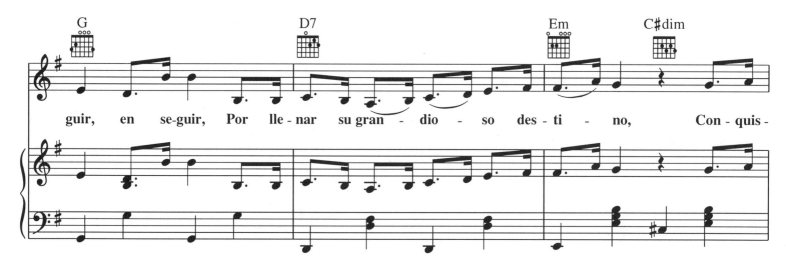

yor. Y con fe in-que-bran-ta - ble el ca - mi - no ___ Del pro-gre-so se a-fa-na en se-

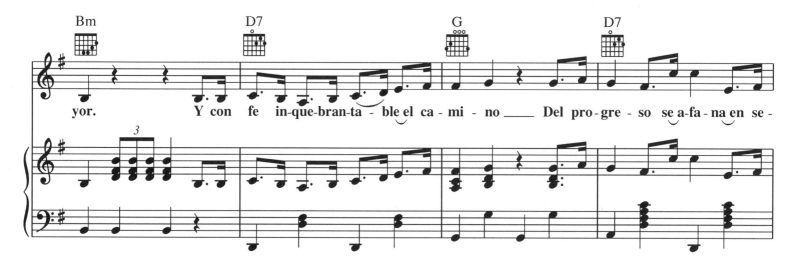

guir, en se-guir, Por lle-nar su gran - dio - so des - ti - no, Con-quis-

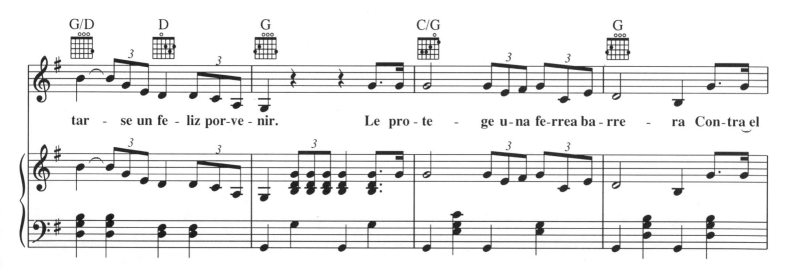

tar - se un fe - liz por-ve - nir. Le pro-te - ge u-na fe-rrea ba-rre - ra Con-tra el

English Translation

We salute the fatherland, with the pride its sons can command.
And we swear with our lives
To tirelessly defend its well-being.
Peace in the name of the Savior.
"El Salvador" rang out, ever-noble.
The pursuit of peace is the eternal mission,
To conserve it is the highest glory.
With unbreakable faith, the road to progress leads us on
To fill our grand destiny,
To ensure a happy future.
A strong barrier protects against the ruin of infidelity.
Since the day the flag flew high,
With blood is written "Liberty!"

ESTONIA
Mu isamaa, mu õnn ja rõõm

Words by JOHANN VOLDEMAR JANSSEN
Music by FREDRIK PACIUS

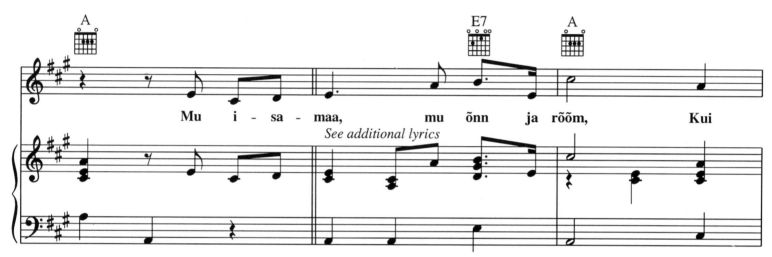

Mu i - sa - maa, mu õnn ja rõõm, Kui

See additional lyrics

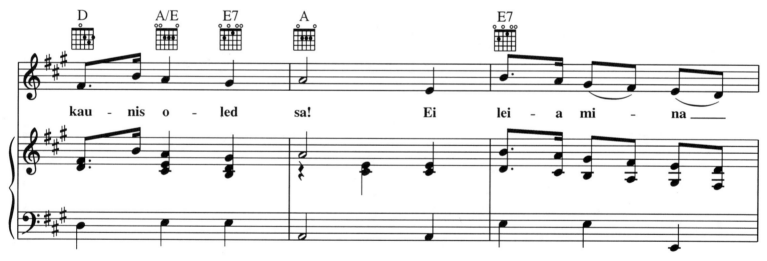

kau - nis o - led sa! Ei lei - a mi - na

ii - al tääl See suu - re lai - a il - ma pääl, Mis

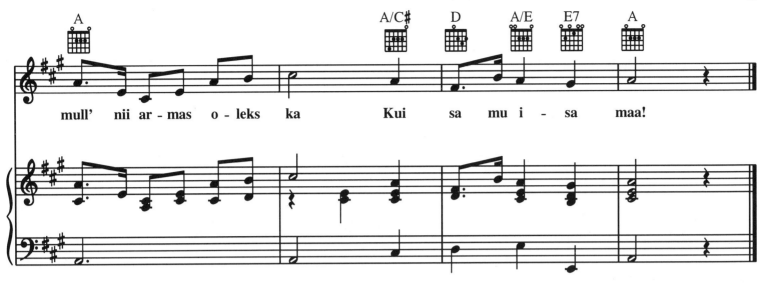

mull' nii ar - mas o - leks ka Kui sa mu i - sa maa!

Additional Lyrics

2. Sa oled mind ju sünnitand
   Ja üles kasvatand!
   Sind tänan mina alati
   Ja Jään sull' truuiks surmani!
   Mull' kõige armsam oled sa,
   Mu kallis isamaa!

3. Su üle Jumal valvaku,
   Mu armas isamaa!
   Ta olgu sinu kaitseja
   Ja võtku rohkest õnnista;
   Mis iial ette võtad sa,
   Mu kallis isamaa!

English Translation

1. My native land, my pride and joy,
   How wondrous fair thou art!
   Where'er I go by land or sea,
   I find no land so dear to me.
   Through all my life I'll cherish thee,
   My own dear native land!

2. It was thou who gavest birth to me,
   Who reared me for thine own.
   To thee I'll ever thankful be
   And vow till death my loyalty.
   Thou art the land most loved by me,
   My own dear native land!

3. God hold His vigil over thee,
   My dearest native land,
   And hold thee in His faithful care,
   Be near when days are dark or fair,
   And bless thine efforts everywhere,
   My own dear native land!

FINLAND
Maamme

Words by JOHAN LUDVIG RUNEBERG
Music by FREDRIK PACIUS

Slow and majestically

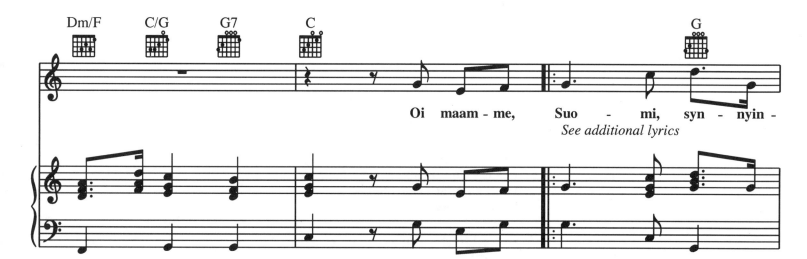

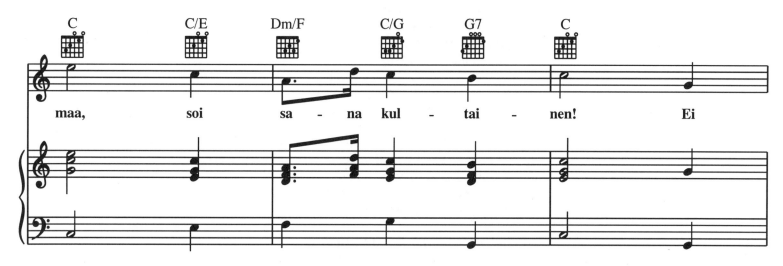

Oi maam - me, Suo - mi, syn - nyin-
See additional lyrics

maa, soi sa - na kul - tai - nen! Ei

laak - so - a, ___ ei ___ kuk - ku - laa, ei vet - tä, ran - taa ___

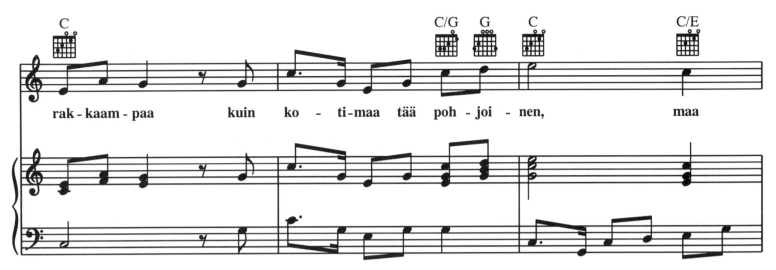

rak - kaam - paa   kuin   ko - ti - maa tää   poh - joi - nen,   maa

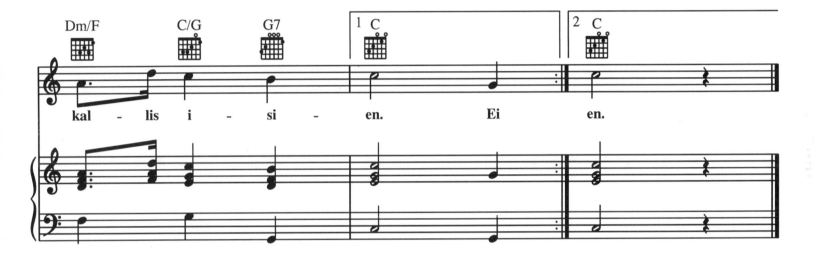

kal - lis   i - si - en.   Ei   en.

Additional Lyrics

2. **Sun kukoistukses kuorestaan**
   kerrankin puhkeaa;
   viel' lempemme saa nousemaan
   sun toivos, riemus loistossaan,
   ja kerran laulus, synnyinmaa,
   korkeemman kaiun saa.
   Viel' lempemme saa nousemaan
   sun toivos, riemus loistossaan,
   ja kerran laulus, synnyinmaa,
   korkeemman kaiun saa.

English Translation

1. **Our land, our land, our native land,**
   Oh, let her name ring clear!
   No peaks against the heavens that stand,
   No gentle dales or foaming strand
   Are loved as we our home revere,
   The earth our sires held dear.
   No peaks against the heavens that stand,
   No gentle dales or foaming strand
   Are loved as we our home revere,
   The earth our sires held dear.

2. **The flowers in their buds that grope**
   Shall burst their sheaths with spring.
   So from our love to bloom shall ope
   Thy gleam, thy glow, thy joy, thy hope,
   And higher yet some day shall ring
   The patriot-song we sing.
   So from our love to bloom shall ope
   Thy gleam, thy glow, thy joy, thy hope,
   And higher yet some day shall ring
   The patriot-song we sing.

FRANCE
La Marseillaise

Words and Music by
CLAUDE-JOSEPH ROUGET de L'ISLE

See additional lyrics

Al-lons, en-fants de la Pa-tri - e, Le jour de gloire est ar-ri-

vé; Con-tre nous de la ty-ran-ni e, L'é-ten-

dard san-glant est le-vé, L'é-ten-dard ___ san-glant est le-

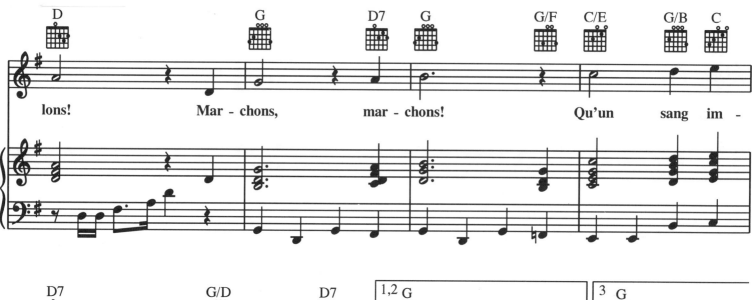

lons!   Mar - chons,   mar - chons!   Qu'un   sang im -

pur   a - breu - ve nos sil - lons!   A-mour Sa - lons!

Additional Lyrics

2. Amour Sacré de la Patrie,
   Conduis, soutiens, nos bras vengeurs.
   Liberté, liberté chérie
   Combats avec tes défenseurs!
   Combats avec tes défenseurs!
   Sous nos drapeaux, que la victoire
   Accours à tes mâles accents!
   Que tes ennemis expirants
   Voient ton triomphe et notre gloire.
      Aux armes, etc.

3. Nous entrerons dans la carrière
   Quand nos aînés n'y seront plus.
   Nous y trouverons leur poussière
   Et la trace de leurs vertus,
   Et la trace de leurs vertus,
   Bien moins jaloux de leur survivre
   Que de partager leur cercueil
   Nous aurons le sublime orgueil
   De les venger ou de les suivre.
      Aux armes, etc.

English Translation

1. Arise you children of our Motherland,
   Oh now is here our glorious day!
   Over us the bloodstained banner
   Of tyranny holds sway!
   Of tyranny holds sway!
   Oh, do you hear there in our fields
   The roar of those fierce fighting men?
   Who came right here into our midst
   To slaughter sons, wives and kin.
      To arms, oh citizens!
      Form up in serried ranks!
      March on, march on!
      And drench our fields
      With their tainted blood!

2. Supreme devotion to our Motherland,
   Guides and sustains avenging hands.
   Liberty, oh dearest Liberty,
   Come fight with your shielding bands.
   Come fight with your shielding bands!
   Beneath our banner come, oh Victory,
   Run at your soul-stirring cry.
   Oh come, come see your foes now die,
   Witness your pride and our glory.
      To arms, etc.

3. Into the fight we too shall enter,
   When our fathers are dead and gone,
   We shall find their bones laid down to rest,
   With the fame of their glories won,
   With the fame of their glories won!
   Oh, to survive them care we not,
   Glad are we to share their grave,
   Great honor is to be our lot
   To follow or to venge our brave.
      To arms, etc.

GUATEMALA
¡Guatemala feliz!

Words JOSÉ JOAQUÍN PALMA
Music by RAFAEL ALVAREZ

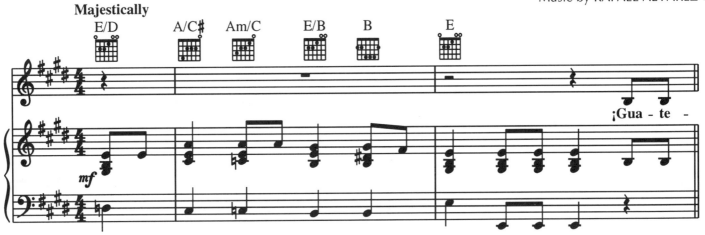

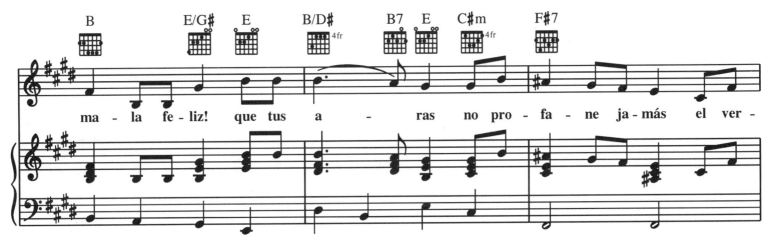

¡Gua - te - ma - la fe - liz! que tus a - ras no pro - fa - ne ja - más el ver -

du - go; ni ha-ya es - cla - vos que la-man el yu - go ni ti -

ra - nos que es-cu - pan tu faz. Si ma - ña - na tu sue - lo sa -

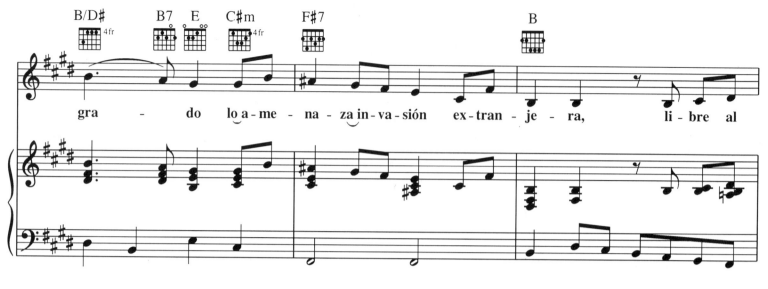

gra - do lo a-me-na-za in-va-sión ex-tran - je - ra, li-bre al

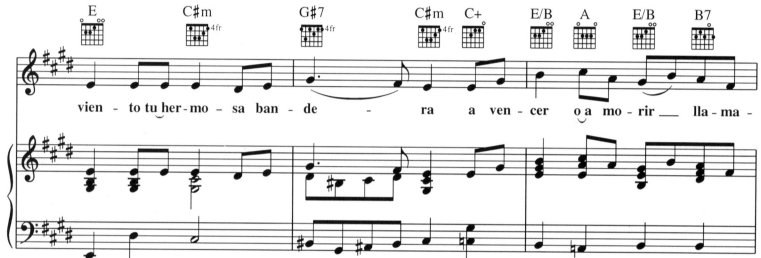

vien - to tu her-mo - sa ban-de - ra a ven-cer o a mo-rir ___ lla-ma-

rá. Li-bre al vien - to tu her-mo - sa ban-de - ra a ven-

cer o a mo-rir lla-ma-rá; que tu pue-blo con á - ni-ma

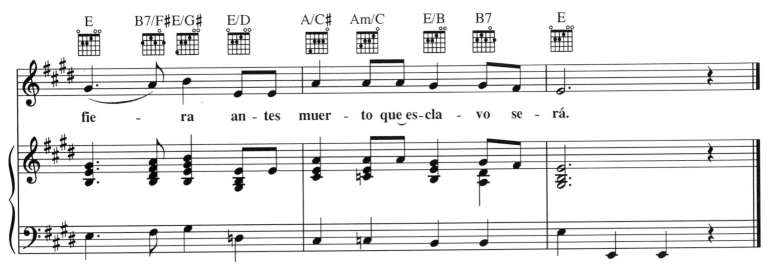

fie - ra an - tes muer - to que es-cla - vo se - rá.

English Translation

Happy Guatemala!
The hangman won't profane your altars.
There are neither slaves nor tyrants that can escape you.
If tomorrow a stranger's invasion threatens your sacred ground,
Your beautiful banner will fly free in the wind
With the call to vanquish the enemy or die fighting.
Guatemala will fiercely fight for freedom.

GERMANY
Einigkeit und Recht und Freiheit

Words by AUGUST HEINRICH HOFFMAN von FALLERSLEBEN
Music by FRANZ JOSEPH HAYDN

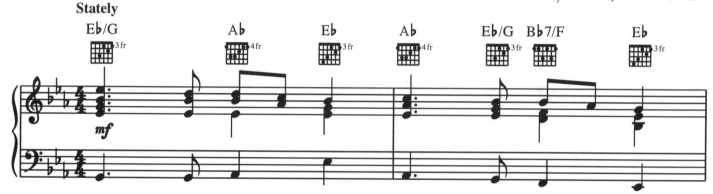

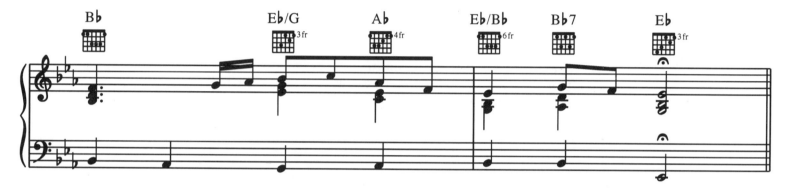

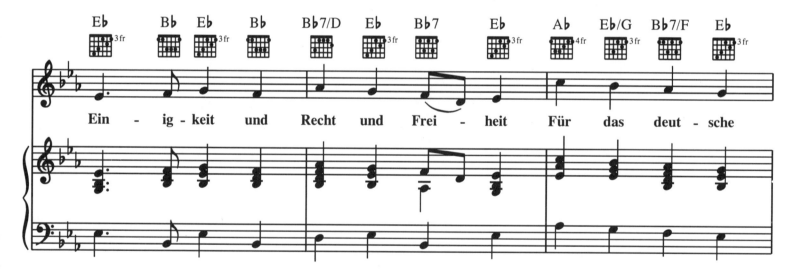

Ein - ig - keit und Recht und Frei - heit Für das deut - sche

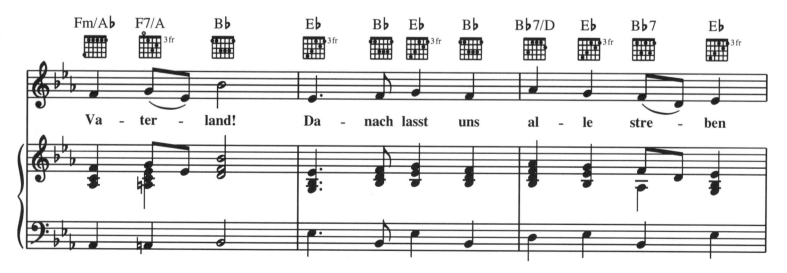

Va - ter - land! Da - nach lasst uns al - le stre - ben

English Translation

Unity and right and freedom
For the German Fatherland,
For this let us all fraternally
Strive each with heart and hand.

Unity and right and freedom
Are the pledge of happiness.
Bloom in the splendor of this happiness,
Germany, our Fatherland.

GREAT BRITAIN
God Save The Queen

Author and Composer Unknown

Nobly

God save our gra - cious Queen;
Thy choic - est gifts in store

Long live our no - ble Queen; God save the Queen!
On her be pleased to pour; Long may she reign;

Send her vic - to - ri - ous, Hap - py and glo - ri - ous,
May she de - fend our laws, And ev - er give us cause

Long to reign o - ver us: God save the Queen!
To sing with heart and voice, God save the Queen!

ITALY
Inno di Mameli

Words by GOFFREDO MAMELI
Music by MICHELE NOVARO

Moderately

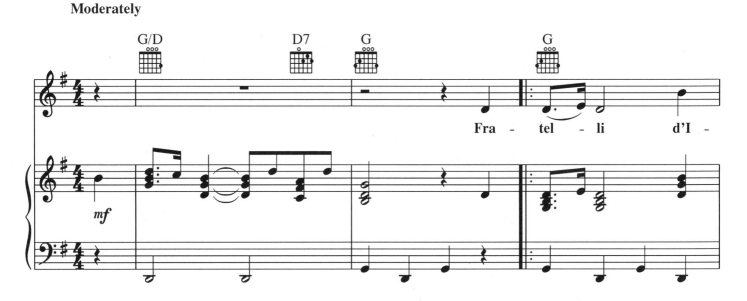

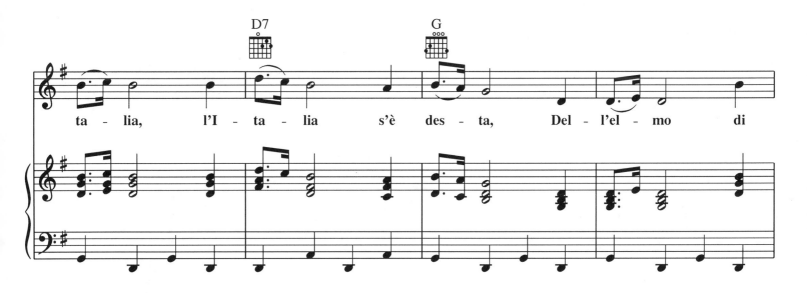

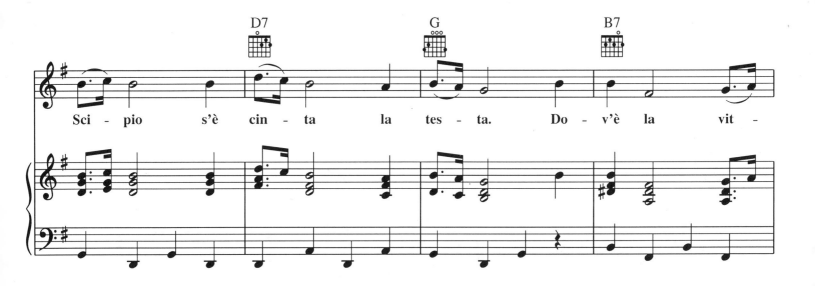

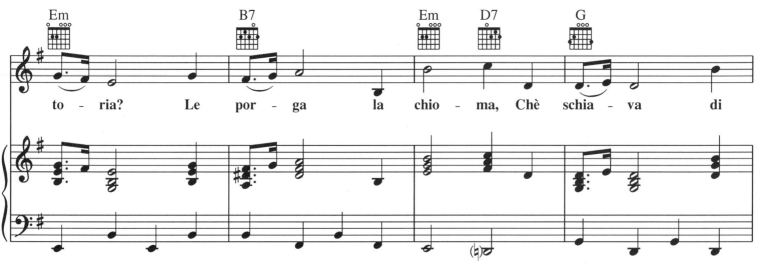

to - ria? Le por - ga la chio - ma, Chè schia - va di

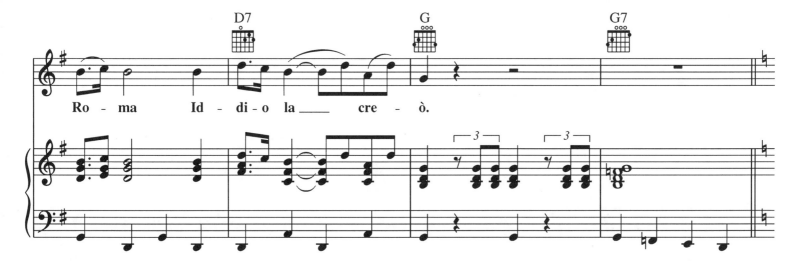

Ro - ma Id - di - o la ___ cre - ò.

Fra - tel - li d'I - ta - lia, l'I - ta - lia s'è des - ta, Dell 'el - mo di

Sci - pio s'è cin - ta la tes - ta. Dov'è la vit - to - ria? Le por - ga la chio - ma, Chè schia - va di

English Translation

Brothers of Italy,
Italy has awakened,
With Scipio's helmet
She has adorned her head.
Where is victory?
She must bow her head to Italy
As God created her
A slave to Rome.

Let us fight together.
We are prepared to die.
We are prepared to die.
Italy has called.

GREECE
Segnorizo apo tin kopsi

Words by DIONYSIUS SOLOMOS
Music by NICOLAOS MANTZAROS

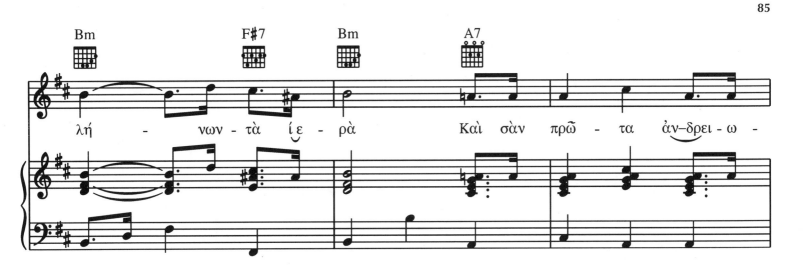

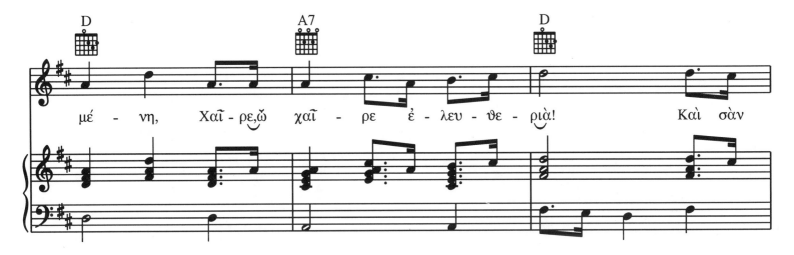

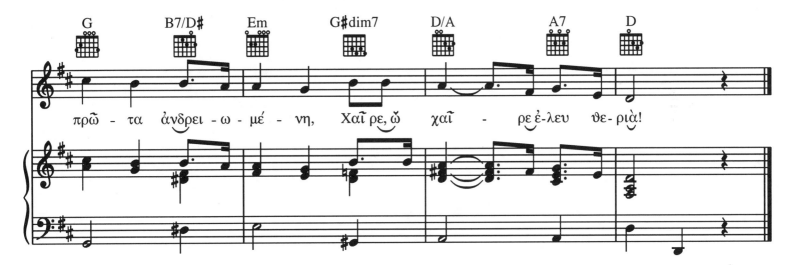

English Phonetics	English Translation
English Phonetics	*English Translation*

Se gnorizo apo tin kopsi
tou spathiou ti tromeri,
se gnorizo apo tin opsi
pou me via metra ti ghi.

Ap ta kokkala vgalmeni
ton Ellinon ta iera
ke san prota andriomeni
Here, Oh Here Eleftheria.

Well I know thee by the edge
Of thy terror-striking brand,
Know thee by the piercing glances
That thou dartest o'er the land.

From the sacred ashes rising
Of the Hellenes great and free,
Valiant as in olden ages
Hail, all hail, O Liberty.

GRENADA
Hail! Grenada, Land Of Ours

Words by IRVA BAPTISTE
Music by LOUIS MASANTO JR.

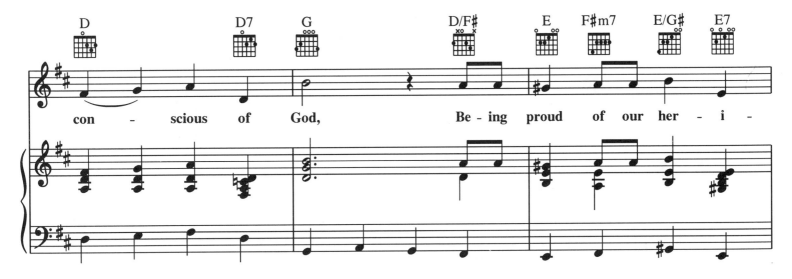

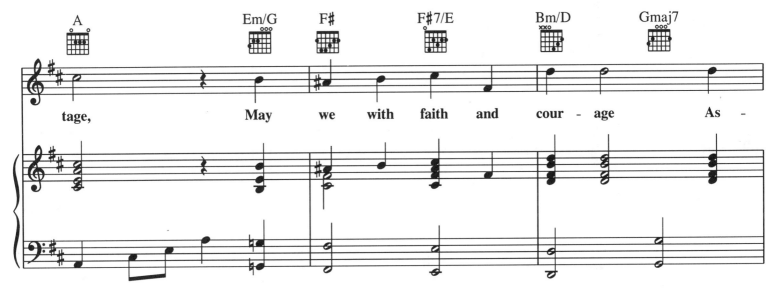

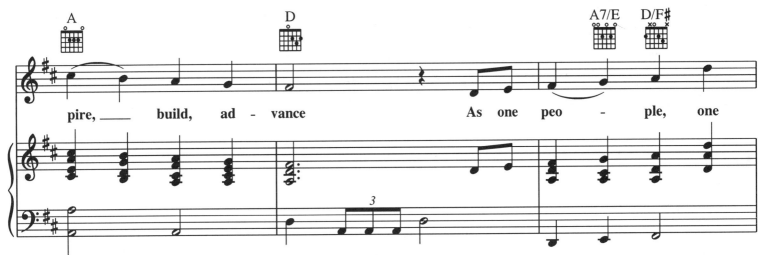

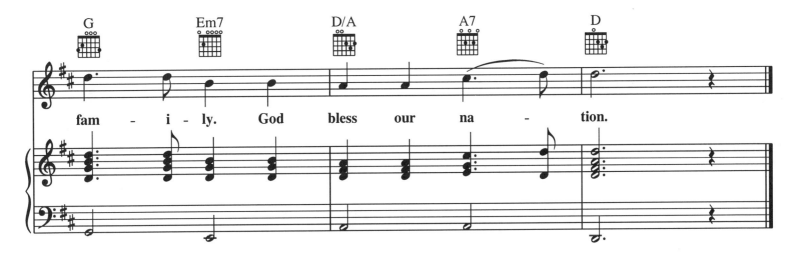

HAITI
La Dessalinienne

Words by JUSTIN LHÉRISSON
Music by NICOLAS GEFFRARD

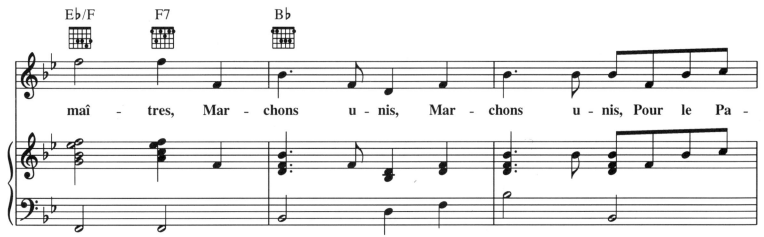

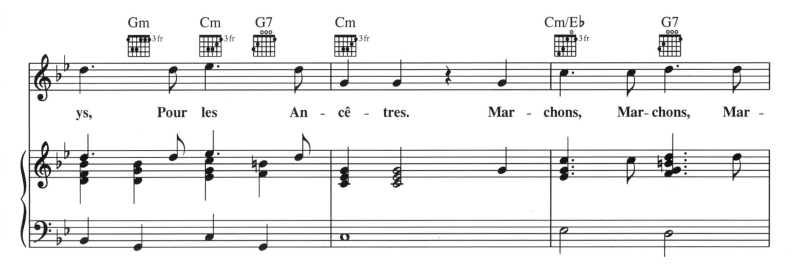

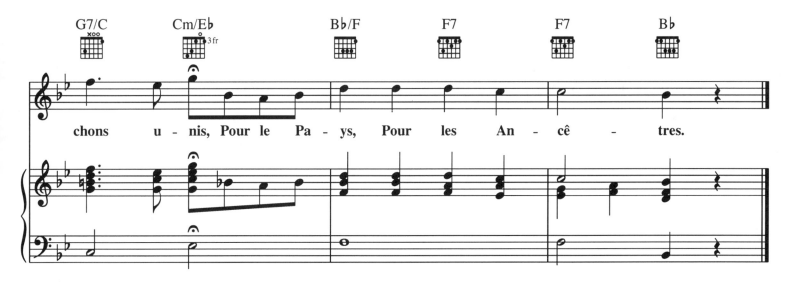

English Translation

For our ancestral home,
We march united, we march united.
We will allow no traitors
To defile this hallowed land.

We march united, we march united
For our ancestral home.
Marching, marching, always united,
For our ancestral home.

HONDURAS
Tu bandera, tu bandera un lampo de cielo

Words by AUGUSTO C. COELLO
Music by CARLOS HARTLING

Moderately

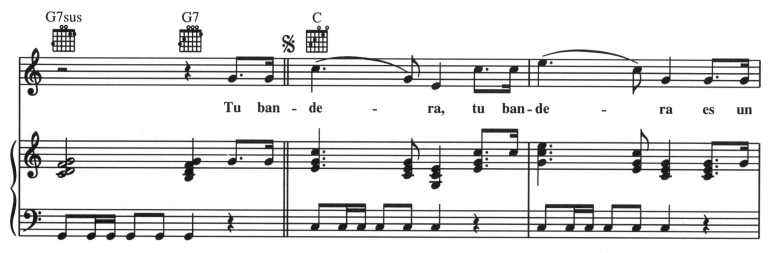

Tu ban-de-ra, tu ban-de-ra es un

lam-po de cie-lo Por un blo-que, por un blo-que de

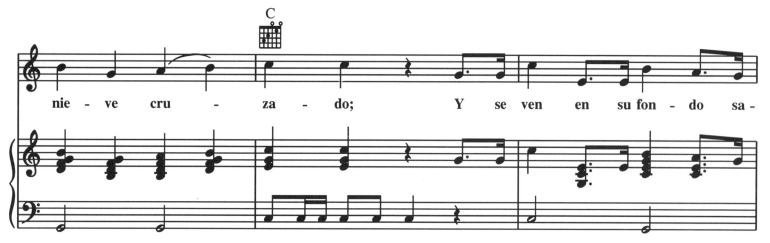

nie-ve cru-za-do; Y se ven en su fon-do sa-

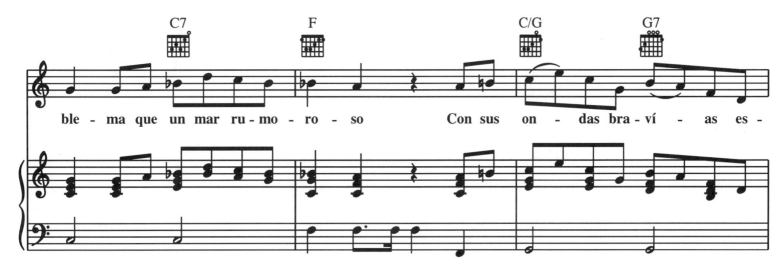

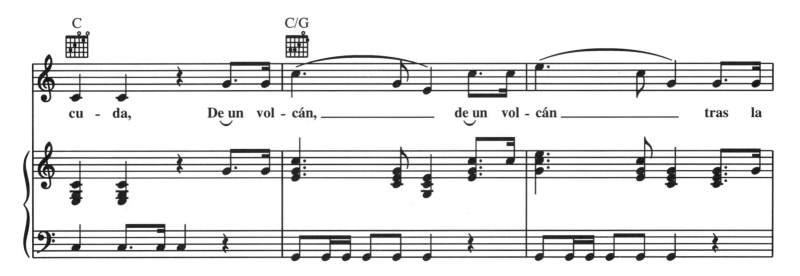

ní - ti - da luz. In - dia vir - gen y her - mo - sa dor -

mí - as De tus ma - res al can - to so - no - ro, Cuan-do e -

cha - da en tus cuen - cas de o - ro El au - daz na - ve-gan - te te ha -

lló; Y al mi - rar tu be - lle - za ex-ta-si - a - do Al in -

English Translation

Your flag is like a light from heaven,
A sacred block of snow crossed by five shining light blue stars.
Your emblem is a rumbling sea
And its brave waves protect from volcano to volcano
Up to the bare summit.
There is a star of sharp light.
Beautiful Indian maiden, you sleep to the song of the sea
With your riches in a river of gold.
The bold explorer discovered your shores.
And upon seeing your beauty,
In ecstacy to the rising tide of your enchantment,
The blue border of your splendid mantle,
With a kiss of love was consecrated.

IRISH REPUBLIC
Amhrán na bhFiann

Moderate march tempo

Words by PEADAR KEARNEY
Music by PATRICK HEENEY

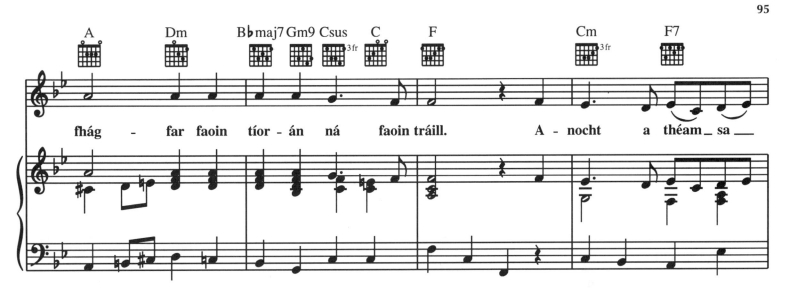

fhág - far faoin tíor - án ná faoin tráill. A - nocht a théam sa

bhear - nabaoil, Le gean ar Ghaeil chun báis nó saoil, Le gun - na scréach, faoi

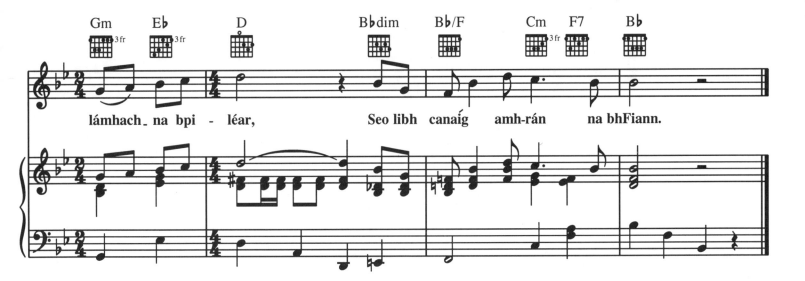

lámhach na bpi - léar, Seo libh canaíg amh-rán na bhFiann.

English Translation

Soldiers are we, whose lives are pledged to Ireland;
Some have come from a land beyond the wave,
Sworn to be free, no more our ancient sireland,
Shall shelter the despot or the slave.
Tonight we man the "bearna baoil."
In Erin's cause, come woe or weal,
'Mid cannon's roar and rifle's peal,
We'll chant a soldier's song.

ISRAEL
Hatiqvah

Words by NAFTALI HERZ IMBER
Music adapted by SAMUEL COHEN

English Translation

So long as still within our breasts
The Jewish heart beats true,
So long as still towards the East,
To Zion, looks the Jew,

So long our hopes are not yet lost—
Two thousand years we cherished them—
To live in freedom in the Land
Of Zion and Jerusalem.

JAMAICA
Eternal Father, Bless Our Land

Words by HUGH SHERLOCK
Music by ROBERT LIGHTBOURNE

Additional Lyrics

2. Teach us true respect for all,
   Stir response to duty's call,
   Strengthen us the weak to cherish,
   Give us vision lest we perish.
   Knowledge send us, Heavenly Father,
   Grant true wisdom from above.

   Chorus

JAPAN
Kimigayo

Author Unknown
Music by HIROMORI HAYASHI

Moderately slow

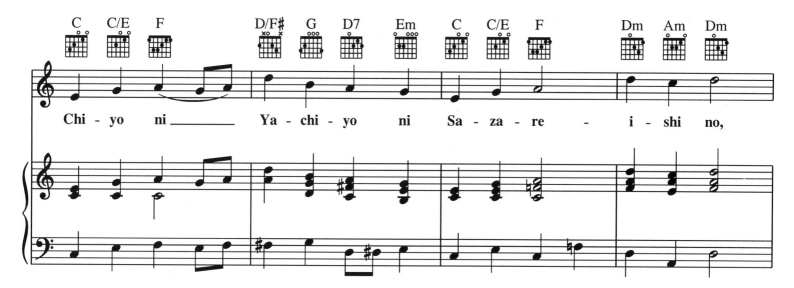

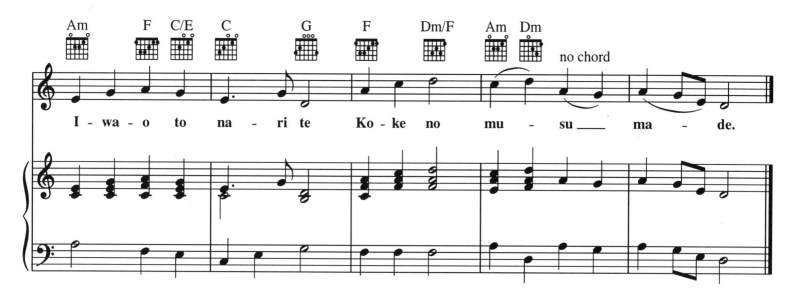

English Translation

Ten thousand years of happy reign be thine:
Rule on, my lord, till what are pebbles now
By ages united to mighty rocks shall grow
Whose venerable sides the moss doth line.

LIBERIA
All Hail, Liberia, Hail!

Words by DANIEL BASHIEL WARNER
Music by OLMSTED LUCA

All hail, Li - be - ria,

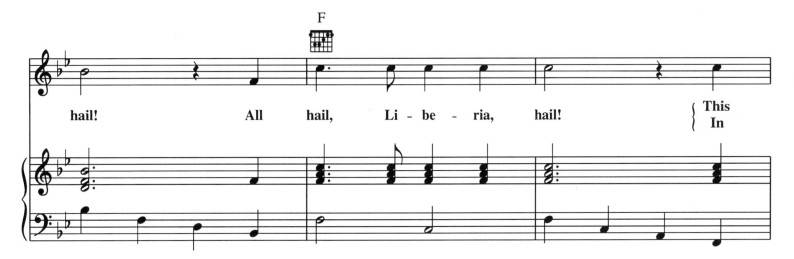

hail! All hail, Li - be - ria, hail! This
In

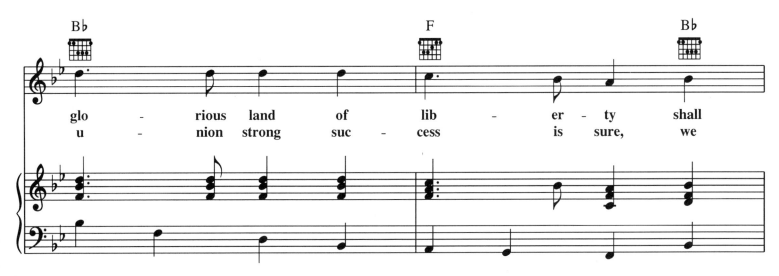

glo - rious land of lib - er - ty shall
u - nion strong of suc - cess is sure, we

LATVIA
Dievs Seveti Latviju

Words and Music by
KARLIS BAUMANIS

Boldly

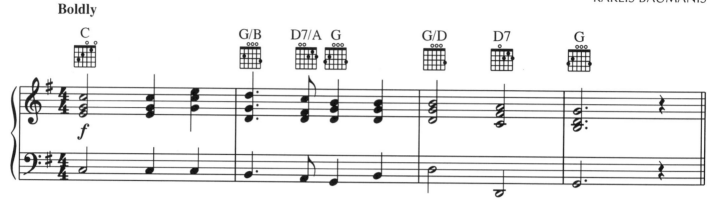

Dievs, svē - ti Lat - vi - ju, Mūs' dār - go tē - vi - ju,

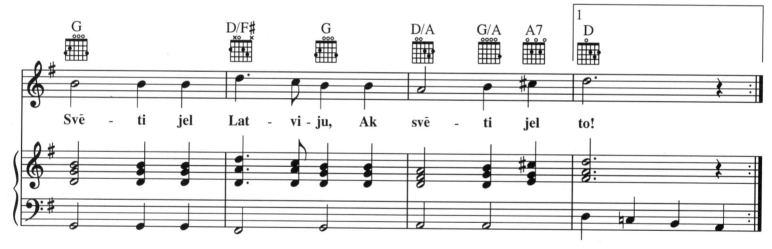

Svē - ti jel Lat - vi - ju, Ak svē - ti jel to!

to! Kur lat - vju mei - tas zied,

English Translation

Bless Latvia, O God,
Our verdant native sod,
Where Baltic heroes trod,
Keep her from harm!
Our blooming daughters near.
Our singing sons appear,
May Fortune smiling here Grace Latvia!

MEXICO

Mexicanos, al grito de guerra

Words by FRANCISCO GONZÁLEZ BOCANEGRA
Music by JAIME NUNÓ

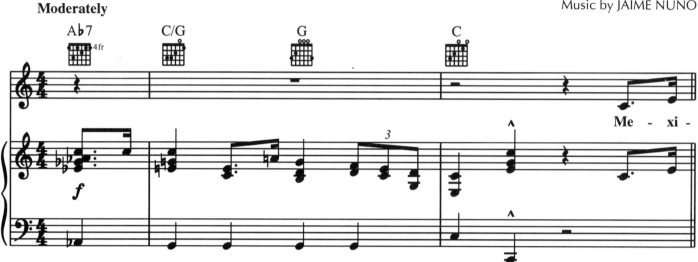

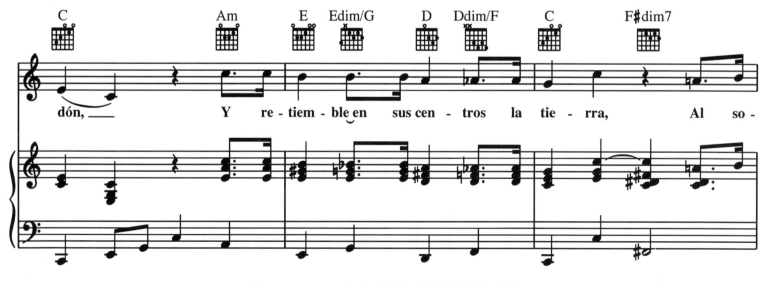

Me - xi -

ca - nos al gri - to ___ de gue ___ rra El a - ce - ro a pres - tad y el bri -

dón, ___ Y re - tiem - ble en sus cen - tros la tie - rra, Al so -

107

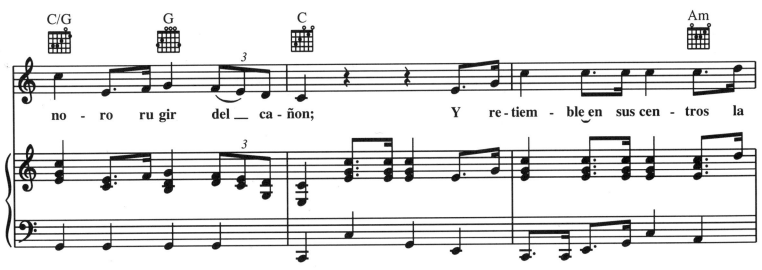

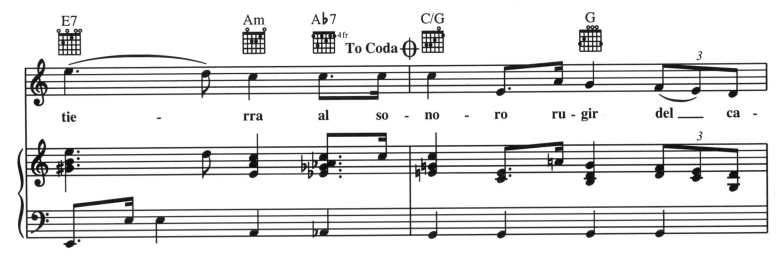

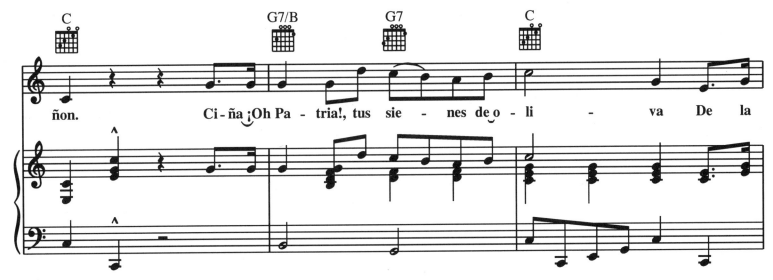

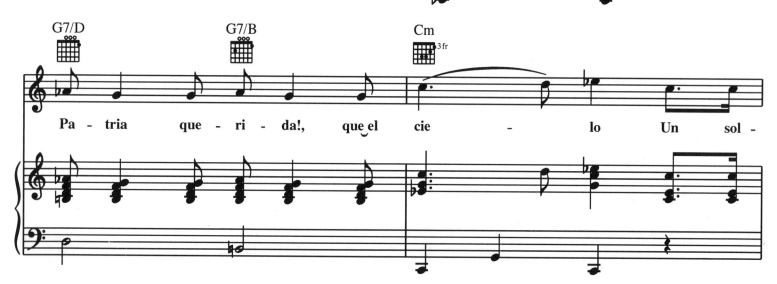

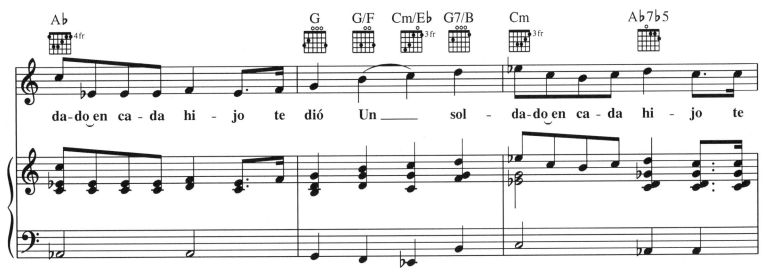

da-do en ca-da hi - jo te dió Un _____ sol - da-do en ca-da hi - jo te

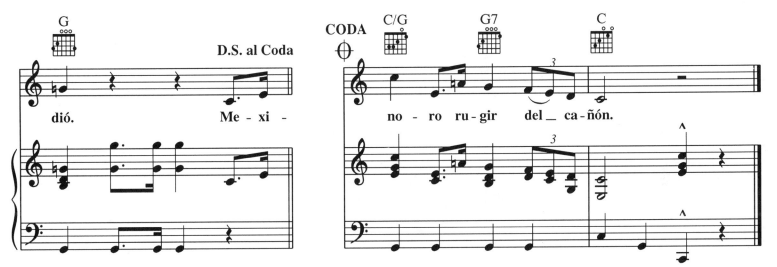

D.S. al Coda

dió.   Me - xi -

CODA

no - ro ru - gir del _ ca - ñón.

English Translation

Mexicans, at the cry of war
Make ready your sword and your horse,
Let the foundations of your land resound
To the sonorous roar of the cannon.

Fatherland! Be crowned with the olive branch
Of peace by the divine archangel,
For in heaven your eternal destiny
Was written by the finger of God.

But if a foreign enemy would dare
To profane your soil with his foot,
Consider, dear Fatherland! That heaven
Has given you a soldier in each son.

NEW ZEALAND
God Defend New Zealand

English Words by THOMAS BRACKEN
Maori Words by THOMAS HENRY SMITH
Music by JOHN JOSEPH WOODS

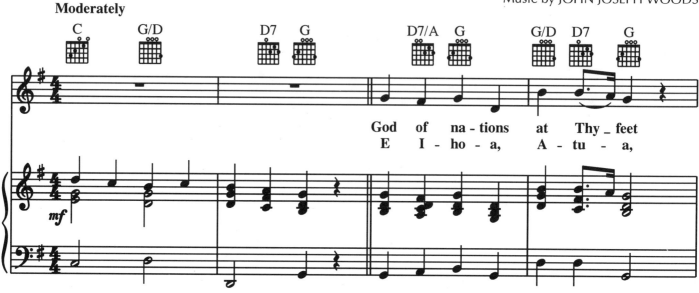

God of na-tions at Thy _ feet
E I - ho - a, A - tu - a,

In the bonds of love _ we _ meet. Hear our voic-es we en-treat, God de-fend our
O nga I - wi! Ma-tou-ra, A ta wha-ka ro-ngo-na; Me a-ro-ha

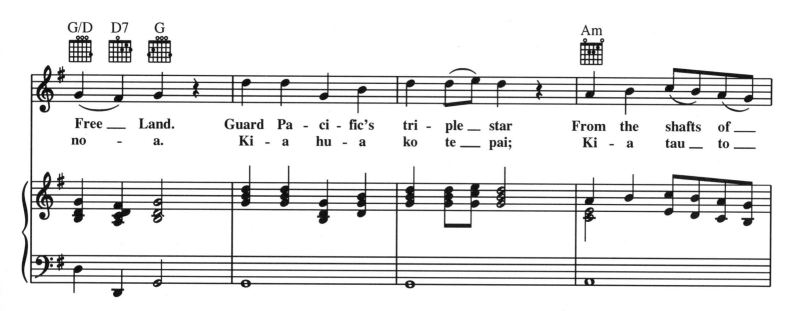

Free __ Land. Guard Pa - ci - fic's tri - ple _ star From the shafts of __
no - a. Ki - a hu - a ko te _ pai; Ki - a tau _ to __

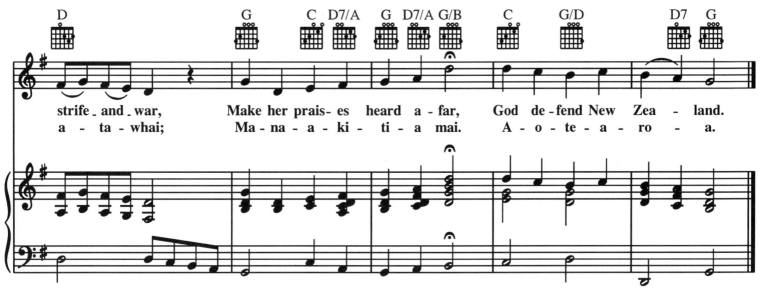

strife _ and _ war,   Make her prais- es   heard a - far,   God de - fend New   Zea - land.
a - ta - whai;   Ma - na - a - ki - ti - a mai.   A - o - te - a - ro - a.

2. Men of every creed and race
   gather here before thy face,
   Asking thee to bless this place,
   God defend our free land.
   From dissension, envy, hate,
   And corruption guard our State,
   Make our country good and great,
   God defend New Zealand.

3. Peace, not war, shall be our boast,
   But, should foes assail our coast,
   Make us then a mighty host,
   God defend our free land.
   Lord of battles in thy might,
   Put our enemies to flight,
   Let our cause be just and right,
   God defend New Zealand.

4. Let our love for thee increase,
   May thy blessings never cease,
   Give us plenty, give us peace,
   God defend our free land.
   From dishonour and from shame,
   Guard our country's spotless name,
   Crown her with immortal fame,
   God defend New Zealand.

5. May our mountains ever be
   Freedom's ramparts on the sea,
   Make us faithful unto thee,
   God defend our free land.
   Guide her in the nation's van,
   Preaching love and truth to man,
   Working out thy glorious plan,
   God defend New Zealand.

2. Ona mano tangata
   Kiri whero, kiri ma,
   Iwi Maori Pakeha,
   Repeke katoa,
   Nei ka tono ko nga he
   Mau e whakaahu ke,
   Kia ora marire
   Aotearoa.

3. Tona mana kia tu!
   Tona kaha kia u;
   Tona rongo hei paku
   Ki te ao katoa
   Aua rawa nga whawhai,
   Nga tutu a tata mai;
   Kia tupu nui ai
   Aotearoa.

4. Waiho tona takiwa
   Ko te ao marama;
   Kia whiti tona ra
   Taiawhio noa.
   Ko te hae me te ngangau
   Meinga kia kore kau;
   Waiho i te rongo mau
   Aotearoa.

5. Tona pai me toitu;
   Tika rawa, pono pu;
   Tona noho, tana tu;
   Iwi no Ihoa.
   Kaua mona whakama;
   Kia hau te ingoa;
   Kia tu hei tauira;
   Aotearoa.

NICARAGUA
Salve a tí Nicaragua

Words by SALOMÓN IBARRA MAYORGA
Composer Unknown

English Translation

Hail to you, Nicaragua!
The cannon sounds no more,
And no longer does the blood of our brothers
Stain your glorious flag.
And no longer does the blood of our brothers
Stain your glorious flag.

Heaven has sent peace to this land;
Nothing can impede on your eternal glory.
You are renowned for the labor of your people
And honor is given to you,
And honor is given to you.

NORTH KOREA
(Korean Democratic People's Republic)
Ach'im ûn pinnara

Words by PAK SE YÔNG
Music by KIM WÔN-GYUN

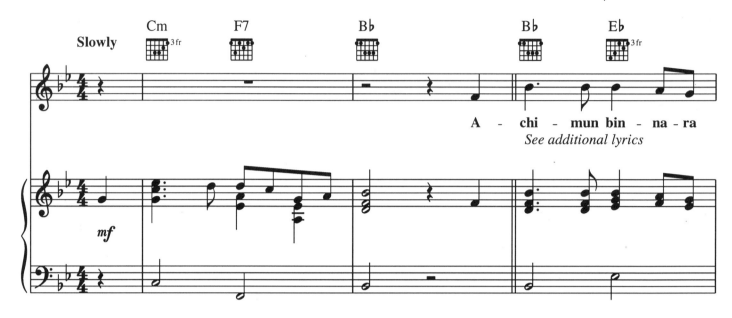

A - chi - mun bin - na - ra
See additional lyrics

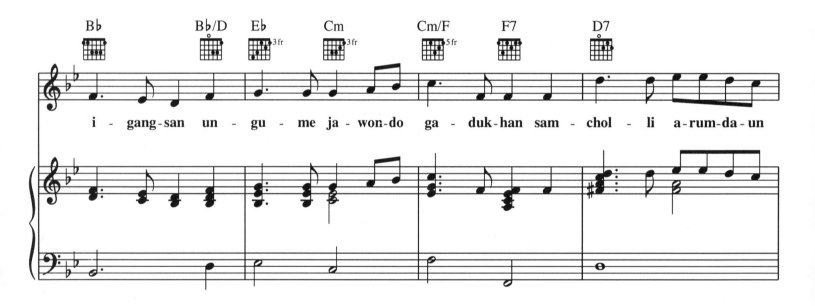

i - gang-san un - gu - me ja - won-do ga - duk-han sam - chol - li a - rum-da - un

nae jo-guk ban - man - nyon o - raen yok-sa - e chal - lan - han mun - hwa-ro

ja - ra - nan sul - gi - ron in - mi - ne   i - yong-gwang mom - gwa - mam da - ba - chyo

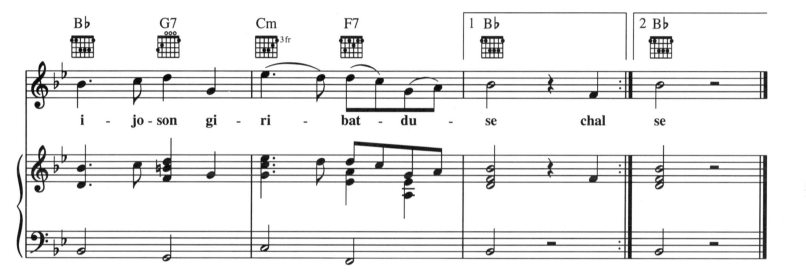

i - jo - son gi - ri - bat - du - se   chal   se

Additional Lyrics

2. Paekdusan gisangul daanggo
   kulloe jongsinun gitduro
   chilliro mungchyojin oksen ddut
   onsegye apso nagari
   sonnun himnododo naemiro
   inmine ddusuro son nara
   hanopsi buganghanun ijoson
   giri binnaese

English Translation

1. Shine bright, you dawn, on this land so fair,
   The country of three thousand *ri,*
   So rich in silver and in gold you are,
   Five thousand years your history.
   Our people ever were renowned and sage,
   And rich in cultural heritage,
   And as with heart and soul we strive,
   Korea shall forever thrive!
   Our people ever were renowned and sage,
   And rich in cultural heritage,
   And as with heart and soul we strive,
   Korea shall forever thrive!

2. And in the spirit of Mount Paekdu,
   With love of toil that shall never die,
   With will of iron fostered by the truth,
   We'll lead the whole world by and by.
   We have the might to foil the angry sea,
   Our land more prosperous still shall be,
   As by the people's will we strive,
   Korea shall forever thrive!
   We have the might to foil the angry sea,
   Our land more prosperous still shall be,
   As by the people's will we strive,
   Korea shall forever thrive!

NORWAY
Ja, vi elsker

Words by BJORNSTJERNE BJORNSON
Music by RIKARD NORDRAAK

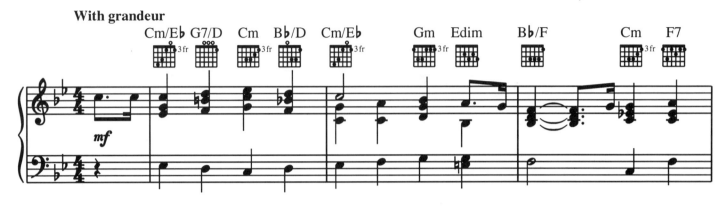

With grandeur

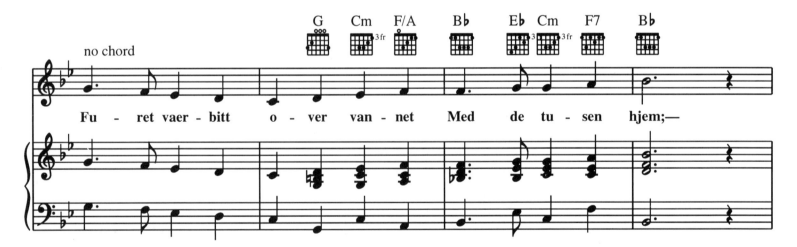

no chord

Ja, vi els - ker det - te lan - det, Som det sti - ger frem

See additional lyrics

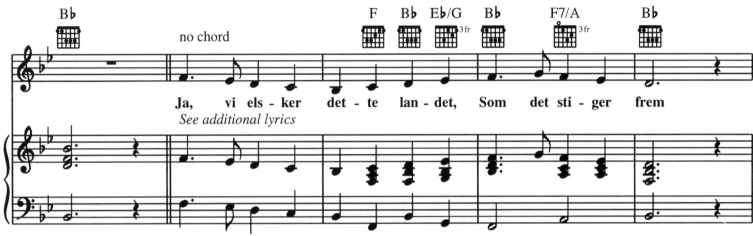

no chord

Fu - ret vaer - bitt o - ver van - net Med de tu - sen hjem;—

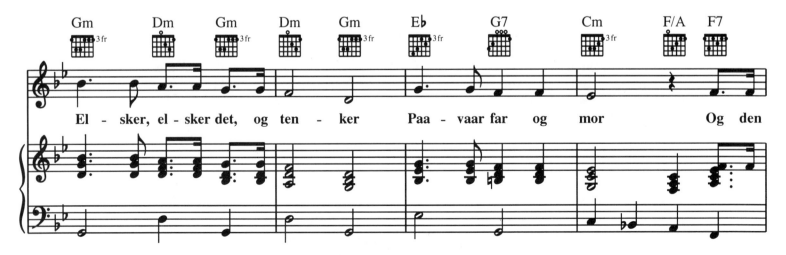

El - sker, el - sker det, og ten - ker Paa - vaar far og mor Og den

Additional Lyrics

2. Norske mann i hus og hytte
   takk din store Gud.
   Landet ville han beskytte
   Skjønt det mørkt sa ut.
   Alt hva fedrene har kjempet,
   mødrene har grætt,
   har den Herre stille lempet
   så vi vant vår rett
   har den Herre stille lempet
   så vi vant vår rett

3. Ja, vi elsker dette landet
   som det stiger frem
   furet, værbitt over vannet
   med de tusen hjem.
   Og som fedres kamp har hevet
   det av ned til seir
   også vi når det blir krevet
   for dets fred slår leir
   også vi når det blir krevet
   for dets fred slår leir

English Translation

1. Yes we love with fond devotion this our land that looms
   Rugged, storm-scarred o'er the ocean, with her thousand homes.
   Love her in our love recalling those who gave us birth.
   And old tales which night in falling brings as dreams to earth,
   And old tales which night in falling brings as dreams as dreams to earth.

2. Norsemen whatso'er thy station thank thy God whose power
   Willed and wrought the land's salvation in her darkest hour.
   All our mothers sought in weeping and our sires in fight
   God has fashioned in his keeping till we gained our right,
   God has fashioned in his keeping till we gained we gained our right.

3. Yes we love with fond devotion this our land that looms
   Rugged, storm-scarred o'er the ocean, with her thousand homes.
   And as warrior sires have made her wealth and fame increase
   At the call we too will aid her armed to guard her peace,
   At the call we too will aid her armed to guard to guard her peace.

PANAMA
Himno Istmeño

Words by JERÓNIMO DE LA OSSA
Music by JORGE A. SANTOS

dien - tes ful - go - res de glo - ria, Se i - lu - mi - na la nue - va Na -

ción. Es pre - ci - so cu - brir con un ve - lo, Del pa -

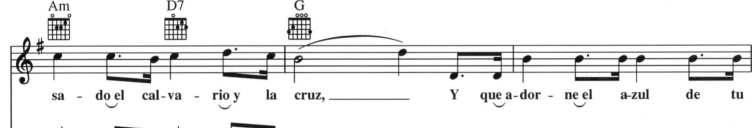

sa - do el cal - va - rio y la cruz, _____ Y que a - dor - ne el a - zul de tu

cie - lo, De con - cor - dia la es - plén - di - da luz. El pro -

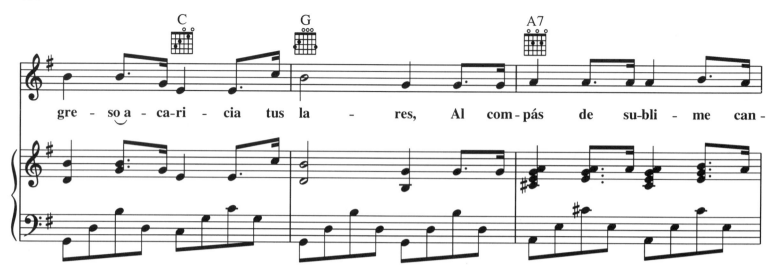

gre - so a - ca-ri - cia tus la - res, Al com - pás de su-bli - me can -

ción; Ves ru - gir a tus pies am - bos ma - res, Que dan

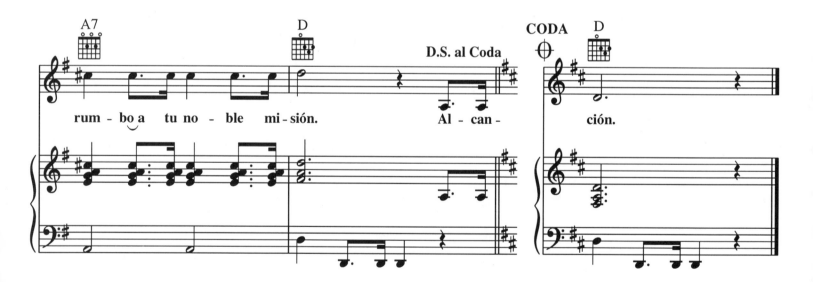

rum - bo a tu no - ble mi - sión. Al - can - ción.

English Translation

**We have finally emerged victorious
In our happy united country.
The new nation shines with burning lights of glory.
Our new nation lights itself up with glory.
We must veil the pains of the past - the Calvary and the cross
To decorate the skies of blue of the future
With harmony and splendid light.
Progress warms the hearth to the rhythm of our sublime song.
Panama - two seas roar at our feet
To add power to your noble mission.**

PERU
¡Somos Libres!

Words by JOSÉ DE LA TORRE UGARTE
Music by JOSÉ BERNARDO ALCEDO

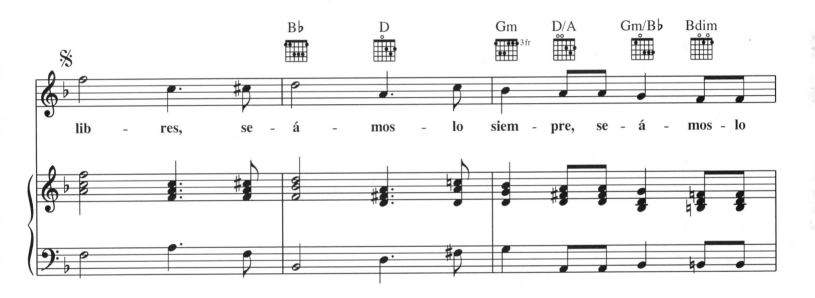

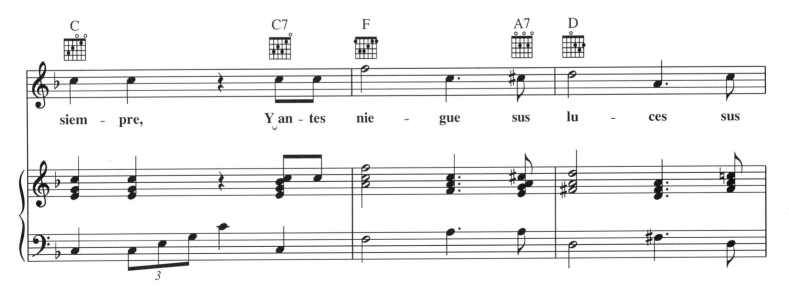

tiem - po en si - len - cio gi - mió. Mas a -

pe - nas el gri - to sa - gra - do ¡Li-ber - tad! en sus cos - tas __

se o - yó, La in-do - len - cia de es-cla - vo sa-cu - de, La hu - mi -

lla - do, la hu - mi - lla - do, la hu - mi -

lla - do cer - viz le - van - tó, _____ La hu - mi - lla - do cer - viz ___ le - van -

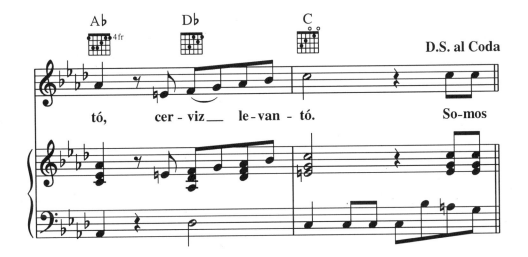

tó,   cer - viz ___ le - van - tó.   So-mos

D.S. al Coda

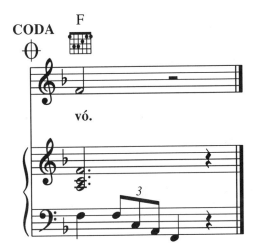

CODA

vó.

English Translation

Freedom is ours, and always will be.
It would be better that the sun should cease to shine
Than for us to fall short of the pledge
Which our nation made to God.

For many years the persecuted people of Peru
Lived in servitude.
Forced to exist as slaves,
For many years their silent cries were not heard.
But then one day the call of freedom
Was heard on Peru's shores.
No longer forced to don the chains of slavery,
The people of Peru could hold their heads high.

Freedom is ours, and will always be.
It would be better that the sun should cease to shine
Than for us to fall short of the pledge
Which our nation made to God.

PARAGUAY

A los pueblos

Words by FRANCISCO ACUÑA DE FIGUEROA
Music by DUPUY

A los pue-blos de A-mé-ri-ca in-fa - us - ta Tres cen-tu-rias un ____ ce-tro o-pri-mió, Mas un dí-a so-ber-bio sur-gien - do, ¡Bas-ta! di-jo, y el

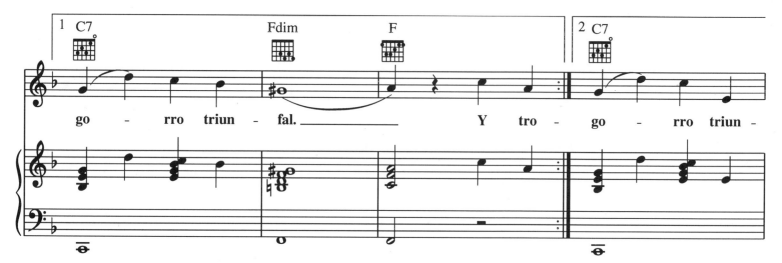

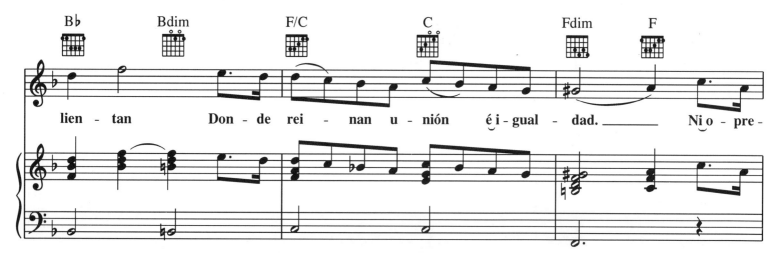

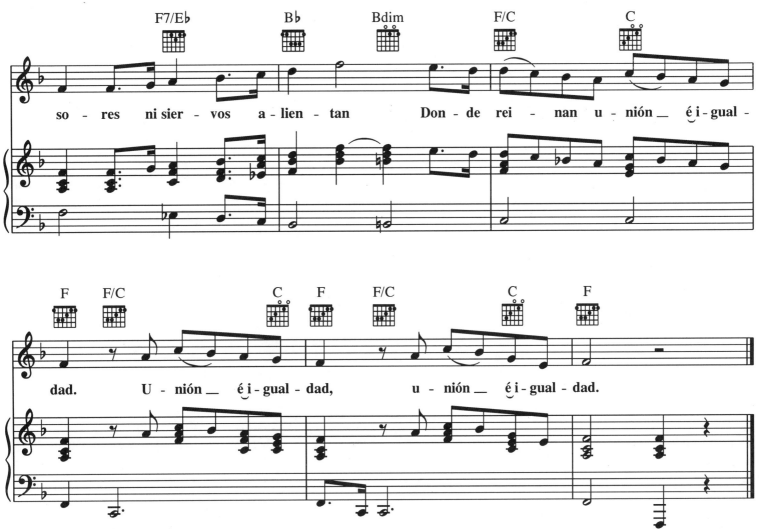

English Translation

For three centuries the people of the Americas
Were oppressed, fearful of demanding their rights.
But then, fearful no longer,
They broke their chains and rose up.

Our ancestors went forth grandly,
Going to their immortal glory.
Breaking the bonds of slavery,
They wore freedom as a glorious crown.
Breaking the bonds of slavery,
They wore freedom as a glorious crown.

Paraguayans, Republic or die!
Our battle will bring freedom.
Slavery cannot exist
Where there is unity and equality.
Slavery cannot exist
Where there is unity and equality,
Where there is unity and equality.

PHILIPPINES
Bayang Magiliw

Words by JOSE PALMA
Music by JULIAN FELIPE

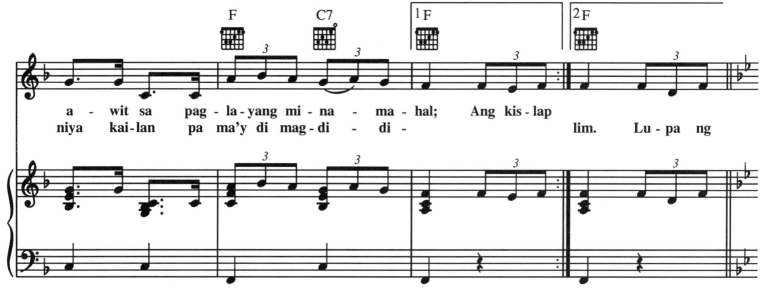

a - wit sa pag-la-yang mi - na - ma - hal; Ang kis-lap

niya kai-lan pa ma'y di mag-di - di - lim. Lu - pa ng

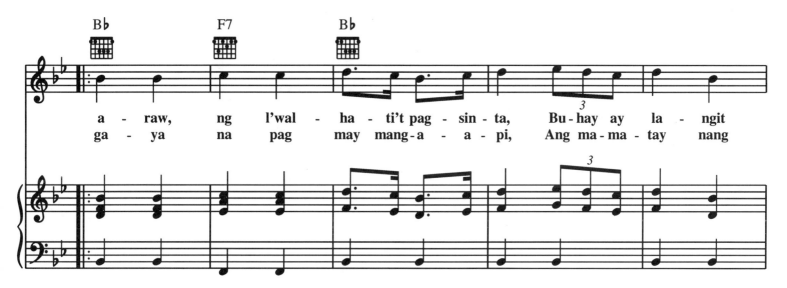

a - raw, ng l'wal - ha - ti't pag - sin - ta, Bu - hay ay la - ngit

ga - ya na pag may mang-a - a - pi, Ang ma - ma - tay nang

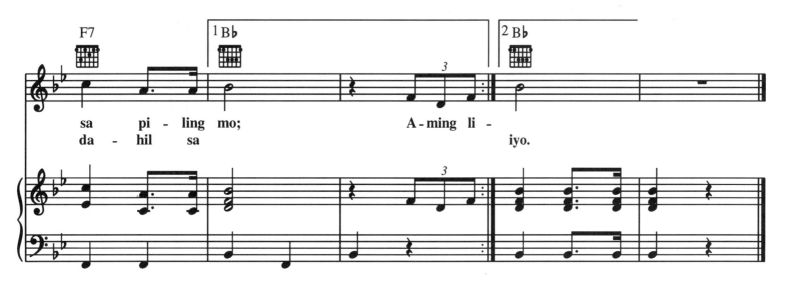

sa pi - ling mo; A - ming li -

da - hil sa iyo.

English Translation

1. **Land of the morning**
   Child of the sun returning
   With fervor burning
   Thee do our souls adore

2. **Land dear and holy**
   Cradle of noble heroes
   Ne'er shall invaders
   Trample thy sacred shore

3. **Ever within thy skies and through thy clouds**
   And o'er thy hills and seas
   Do we behold the radiance, feel the throb
   Of glorious liberty.

4. **Thy banner dear to all our hearts**
   Its sun and stars alight
   Oh, never shall its shining field
   Be dimmed by tyrant's might!

5. **Beautiful land of love, O land of light**
   In thine embrace 'tis rapture to lie.
   But is glory ever, when thou art wronged
   For us, thy sons, to suffer and die.

POLAND
Jeszcze Polska nie zginęla

Words by JÓZEF WYBICKI
Music by MICHAL KLEOFAS OGÍNSKI

Jesz - cze Pol - ska nie zgi - nę - ła, ___ kie - dy my ży - je - my,

Co nam ob - ca prze - moc wzię - ła, ___ szab - lą od - bie - rze - my.

Marsz, marsz, Dą - brow - ski; z zie - mi wło - skiej do Pol - ski!

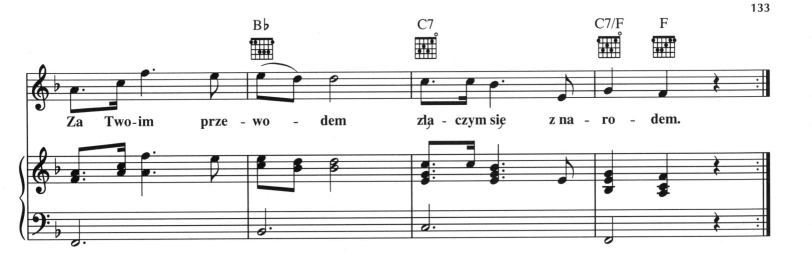

Za Two-im   prze - wo - dem   złą - czym się   z na - ro - dem.

Additional Lyrics

2. Przejdziem Wisłę, przejdziem Wartę, będziem Polakami.
   Dał nam przykład Bonaparte, jak zwyciężać mamy.
   Marsz, marsz, Dąbrowski, z ziemi włoskiej do Polski!
   Za Twoim przewodem złączym się z narodem.

3. Jak Czarniecki do Poznania po szwedzkim zaborze
   Dla ojczyzny ratowania rzucim się przez morze.
   Marsz, marsz, Dąbrowski, z ziemi włoskiej do Polski!
   Za Twoim przewodem złączym się z narodem.

4. Mówił ojciec do swej Basi, smutny, zapłakany:
   "Słuchaj jeno, pono nasi biją w tarabany."
   Marsz, marsz, Dąbrowski, z ziemi włoskiej do Polski!
   Za Twoim przewodem złączym się z narodem.

English Translation

1. Poland will not be lost
   until we live.
   We will fight for everything that our enemies
   had taken from us.

Chorus   March, march Dąbrowski,
   from Italy to Poland!
   Under your command
   we will unite.

2. We will cross the Vistula and Warta Rivers,
   we will be Poles,
   Bonaparte showed us how to win.

   Chorus

3. Like Czarniecki to Poznań
   after Swedish annexation
   we will come back across the sea
   to save our motherland.

   Chorus

4. Father says to his wife Basia in tears:
   "Listen only, apparently our people are
   beating the kettle drums."

   Chorus

RUSSIA
from A Life For The Czar

Music by
MIKHAIL IVANOVICH GLINKA

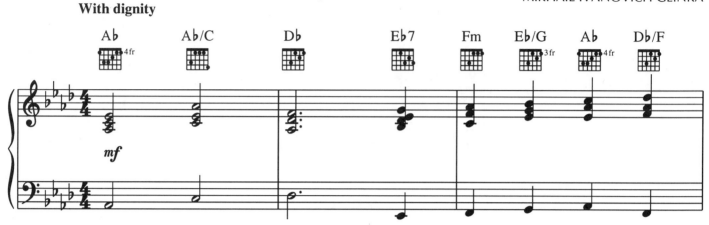

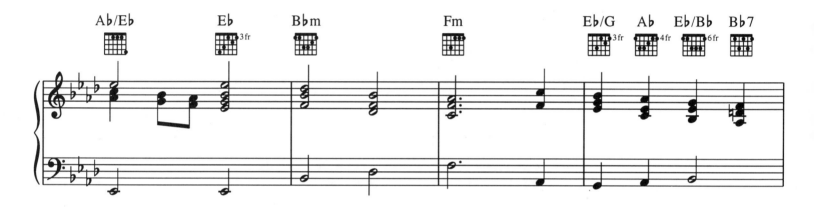

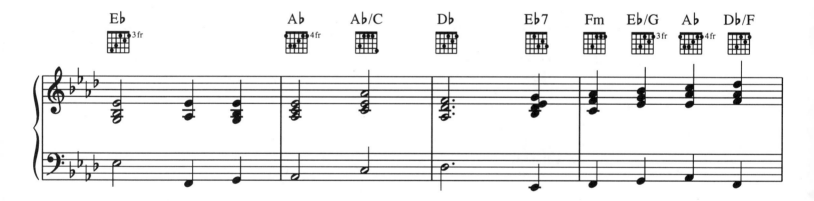

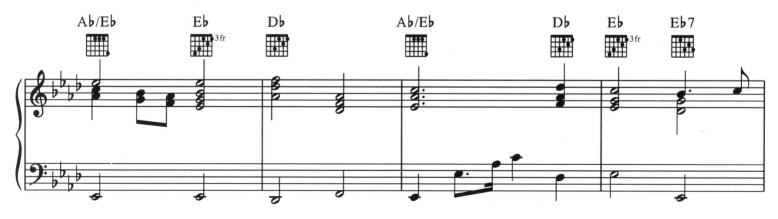

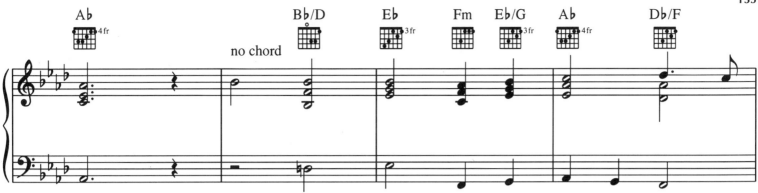

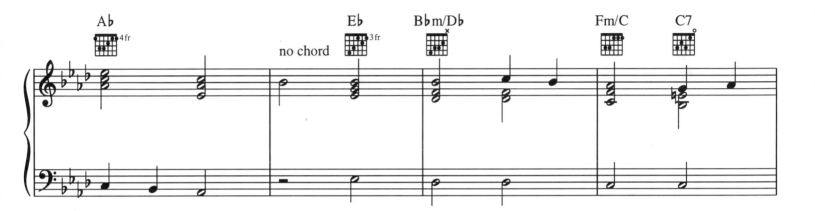

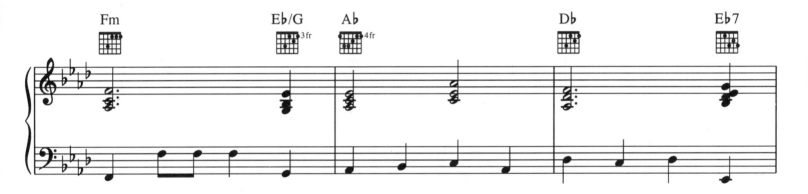

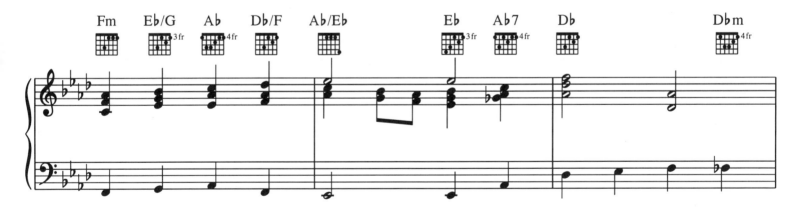

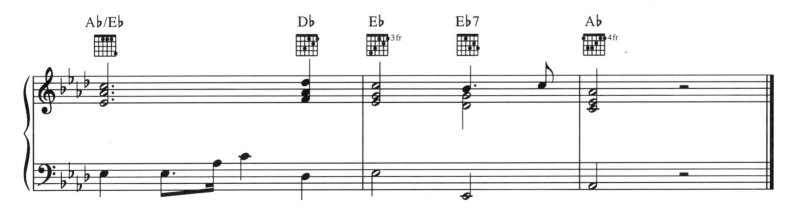

SLOVAKIA
Nad Tatrou Sa Blyska

Words by JANKO MATÚŠKA
Composer Unknown

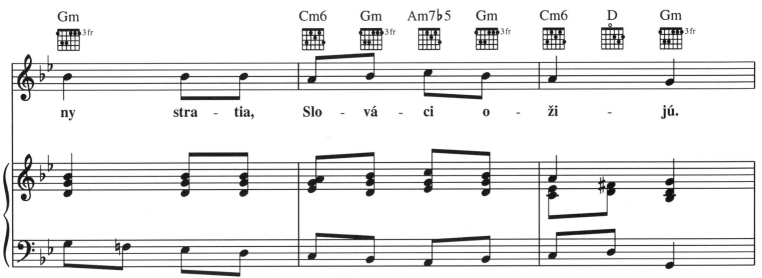

ny   stra - tia,   Slo - vá - ci   o - ži - jú.

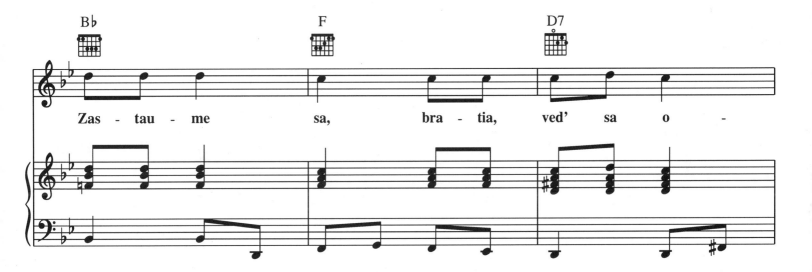

Zas - tau - me   sa,   bra - tia,   ved' sa o -

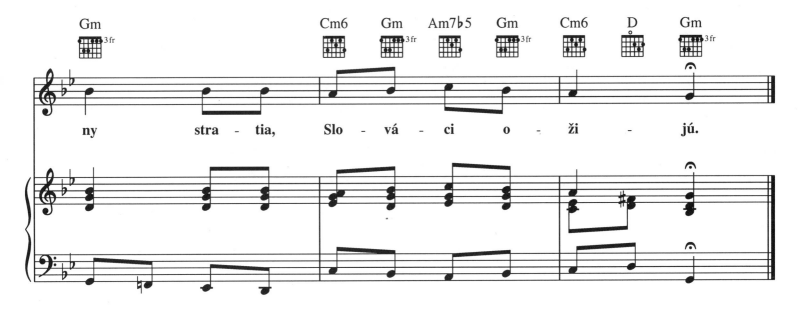

ny   stra - tia,   Slo - vá - ci   o - ži - jú.

English Translation

Over the Tatra mountains, lightning
flashes and thunder claps wildly,
Over the Tatra mountains, lightning
flashes and thunder claps wildly,
Let's stop, brothers, for the thunder will disappear,
Slovaks will live on.
Let's stop, brothers, for the thunder will disappear,
Slovaks will live on.

SOUTH AFRICA
Die Stem van Suid-Afrika

Words by CORNELIS JACOB LANGENHOVEN
Music by MARTHINUS LOURENS de VILLIERS

See additional verses

139

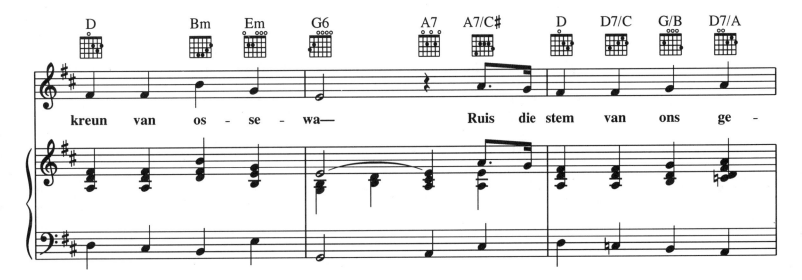

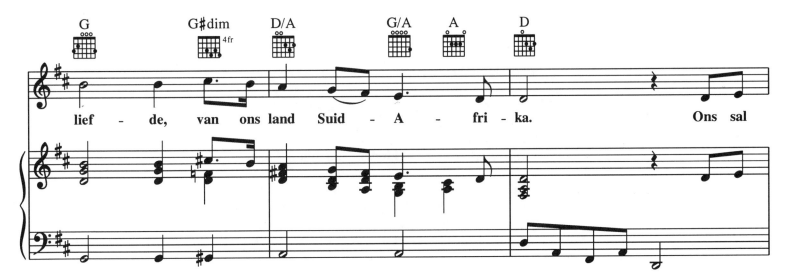

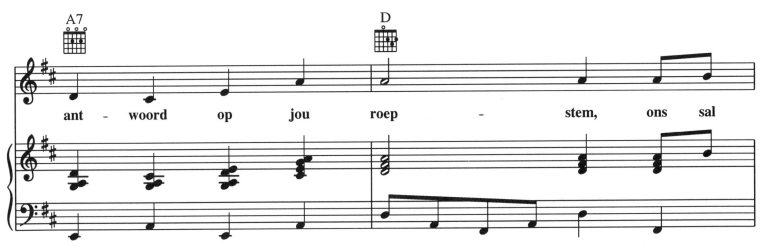

Additional Verses

2. In die merg van ons gebeente, in ons hart en siel en gees,
   In ons roem op ons verlede, in ons hoop op wat sal wees,
   In ons wil en werk en wandel, van ons wieg tot aan ons graf—
   Deel geen ander land ons liefde, trek geen ander trou ons af.
   Vaderland! ons sal die adel van jou naam met ere dra:
   Waar en trou as Afrikaners — kinders van Suid-Afrika.

3. In die songloed van ons somer, in ons winternag se kou,
   In die lente van ons liefde, in die lanfer van ons rou.
   By die klink van huw'liks-klokkies, by die kluitklap op die kis—
   Streel jou stem ons nooit verniet nie, weet jy waar jou kinders is.
   Op jou roep sê ons nooit nee nie, sê ons altyd, altyd ja:
   Om te lewe, om te sterwe — ja, ons kom. Suid-Afrika.

4. Op U Almag vas vertrouend, het ons vadere gebou:
   Skenk ook ons die krag, o Here! om te handhaaf en te hou—
   Dat die erwe van ons vaad're vir ons kinders erwe bly:
   Knegte van die Allerhoogste, teen die hele wêreld vry.
   Soos ons vadere vertrou het, leer ook ons vertrou, o Heer—
   Met ons land en met ons nasie sal dit wel wees, God regeer.

English Version

1. Ringing out from our blue heavens, from our deep seas breaking round;
   Over everlasting mountains where the echoing crags resound;
   From our plains where creaking wagons cut their trails into the earth—
   Calls the spirit of our Country, of the land that gave us birth.
   At thy call we shall not falter, firm and steadfast we shall stand.
   At thy will to live or perish. O South Africa, dear land.

2. In our body and our spirit, in our inmost heart held fast;
   In the promise of our future and the glory of the past;
   In our will, our work, our striving, from the cradle to the grave—
   There's no land that shares our loving, and no bond that can enslave.
   Thou has borne us and we know thee. May our deeds to all proclaim
   Our enduring love and service to thy honour and thy name.

3. In the golden warmth of summer, in the chill of winter's air.
   In the surging life of springtime, in the autumn of despair:
   When the wedding bells are chiming, or when those we love depart,
   Thou dost know us for thy children and dost take us to thy heart.
   Loudly peals the answering chorus: We are thine, and we shall stand.
   Be it life or death, to answer to thy call, beloved land.

4. In Thy power, Almighty, trusting, did our fathers build of old:
   Strengthen then, O Lord, their children to defend, to love, to hold—
   That the heritage they gave us for our children yet may be:
   Bondsmen only to the Highest and before the whole world free.
   As our fathers trusted humbly, teach us, Lord, to trust Thee still:
   Guard our land and guide our people in Thy way to do Thy will.

SOUTH KOREA
(Korean Republic)
Tonghai moolkwa Paiktusani

Author Unknown
Music by EAK TAY AHN

Moo - gung-wha sam - chul - ri Hwa-ryu kang - san,

Tae - han sa-ram tae-han — eu - ro Ki - ri po-chun-ha - sae.

English Translation

Until the East Sea's waves are dry,
(and) Paek-tu-san worn away,
God watch o'er our land forever!
Our Korea manse!

Rose of Sharon, thousand miles
of range and river land!
Guarded by her people, ever may Korea stand!

SPAIN
Marcha real

Composer Unknown

March

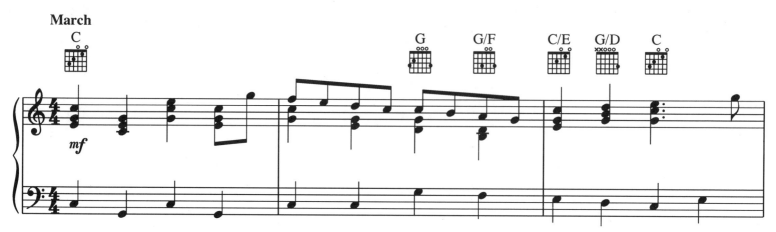

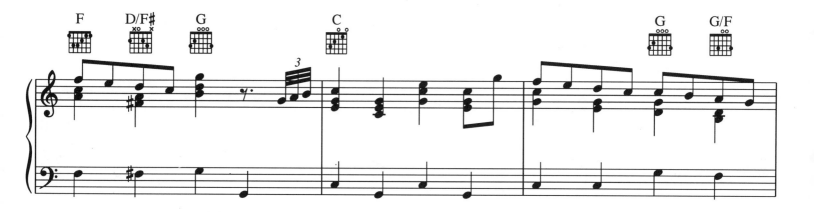

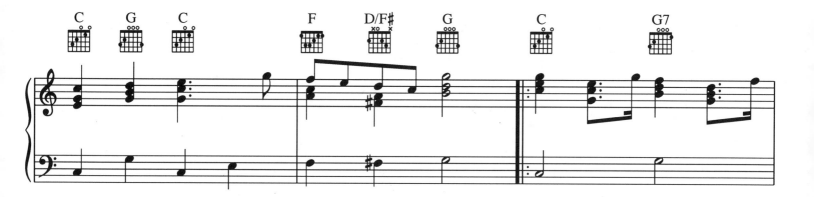

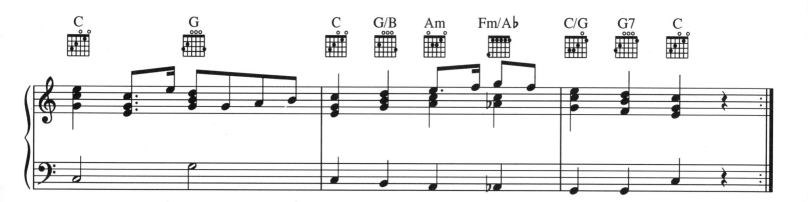

SWITZERLAND
Swiss Psalm

Words by LEONHARD WIDMER
Music by ALBERIK ZWYSSIG

German: Trittst im Mor - gen - rot da - her, seh' ich dich im
French: Sur nos monts, quand le so - leil an - nonce un bril -
Italian: Quan - do bion - da au - ro - ra il mat - tin cin -
Surselvisch: Cu la pez - za bein mar - vegl splen - du - re - scha
Ladinisch: In l'au - ro - ra la da - man at cu - gnuo - scha

Strah - len - meer, dich, du Hoch - er - ha - be - ner, Herr - li -
lant ré - veil, et pré - dit d'un plus beau jour le re -
do - ra, l'al - ma mia t'a - do - ra Re del
dal su - legl: Cat - tel jeu tei a - da - gur, Cre - a -
bain l'u - man, spiert e - tern do - mi - na - tur, Tuot pus -

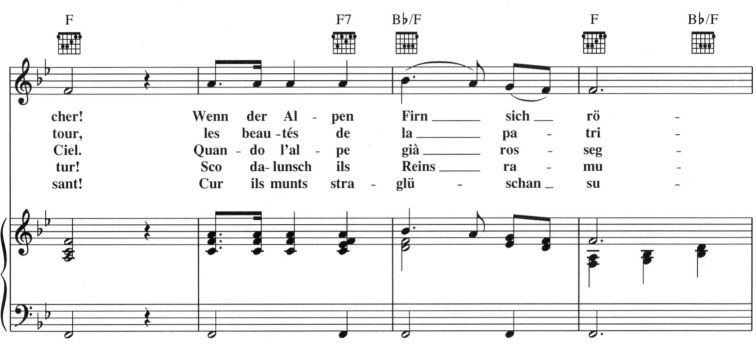

cher! / Wenn der Al - pen Firn _____ sich _____ rö -
tour, / les beau -tés de la _____ pa - tri -
Ciel. / Quan - do l'al - pe già _____ ros - seg -
tur! / Sco da-lunsch ils Reins _____ ra - mu -
sant! / Cur ils munts stra - glü - schan _ su

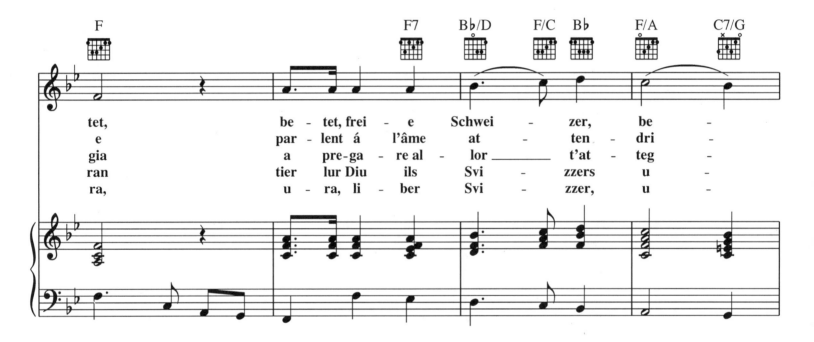

tet, / be - tet, frei - e Schwei - zer, be -
e / par - lent á l'âme at - ten - dri -
gia / a pre-ga - re al - lor _____ t'at - teg -
ran / tier lur Diu ils Svi - zzers u -
ra, / u - ra, li - ber Svi - zzer, u -

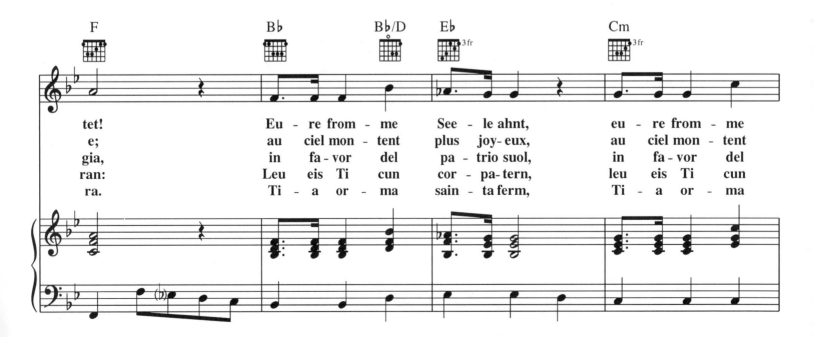

tet! / Eu - re from - me See - le ahnt, eu - re from - me
e; / au ciel mon - tent plus joy-eux, au ciel mon - tent
gia, / in fa - vor del pa - trio suol, in fa - vor del
ran: / Leu eis Ti cun cor - pa-tern, leu eis Ti cun
ra. / Ti - a or - ma sain - ta ferm, Ti - a or - ma

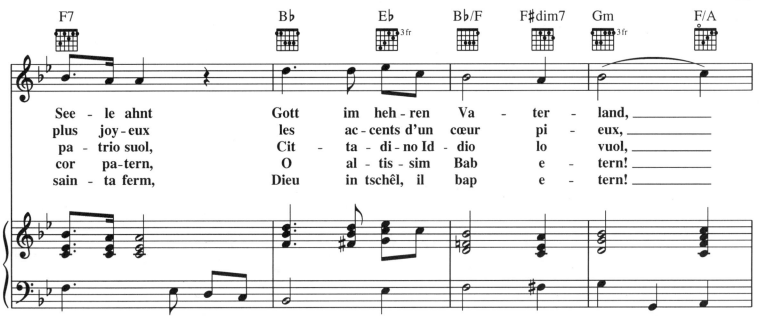

See - le ahnt / plus joy-eux / pa - trio suol, / cor pa-tern, / sain - ta ferm,

Gott / les / Cit / O / Dieu

im heh - ren / ac-cents d'un / ta - di - no Id - / al - tis - sim / in tschêl, il

Va - ter - land, / cœur pi - eux, / dio lo vuol, / Bab e - tern! / bap e - tern!

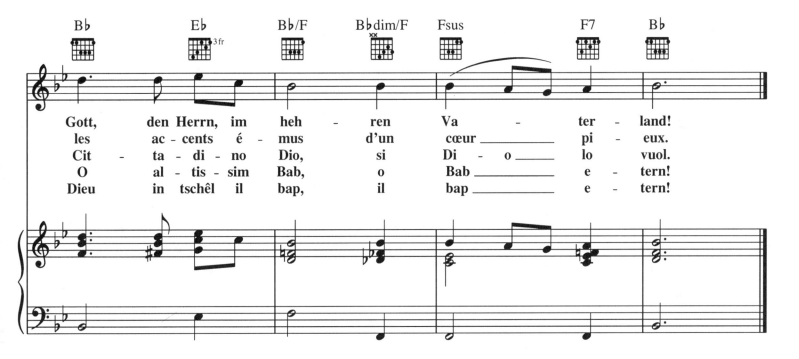

Gott, / les / Cit / O / Dieu

den Herrn, im / ac - cents é - mus / ta - di - no Dio, / al - tis - sim Bab, / in tschêl il bap,

heh - ren / d'un / si / o / il

Va - ter - land! / cœur pi - eux. / Di - o lo vuol. / Bab e - tern! / bap e - tern!

English Translation

Radiant in the morning sky,
Lord, I see Thee; Thou art nigh
Thou, O most illustrious,
Glorious.
When the Alps glow in their splendour,
Pray, ye Swiss, your hearts surrender.
For we sense and understand
God in our Fatherland
God, the Lord, in our Fatherland.

SWEDEN
Du gamla, du fria

Words by RICHARD DYBECK
Composer Unknown

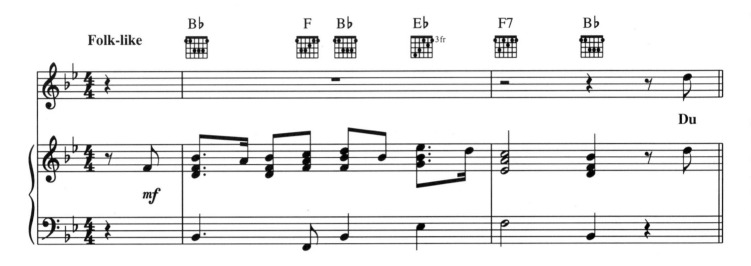

Folk-like

See additional lyrics

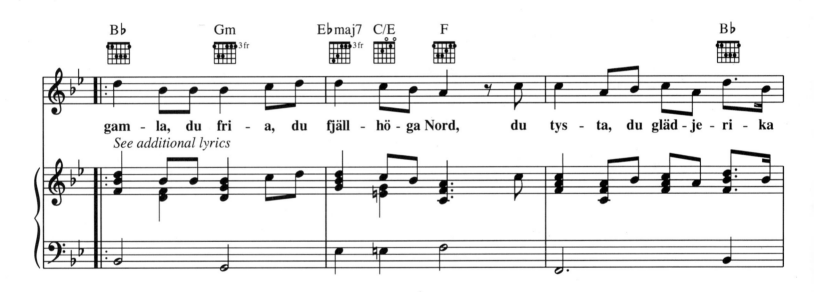

gam - la, du fri - a, du fjäll - hö - ga Nord, du tys - ta, du gläd - je - ri - ka

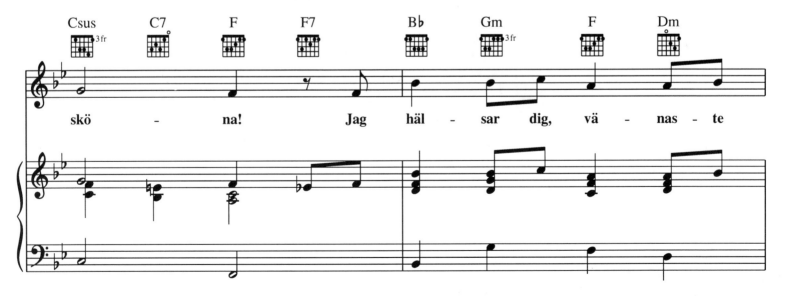

skö - na! Jag häl - sar dig, vä - nas - te

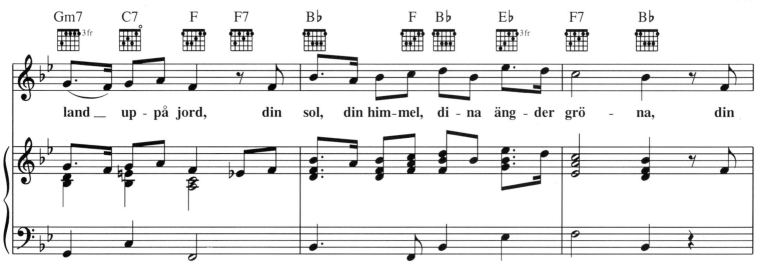

land __ up-på jord, din sol, din him-mel, di-na äng-der grö - na, din

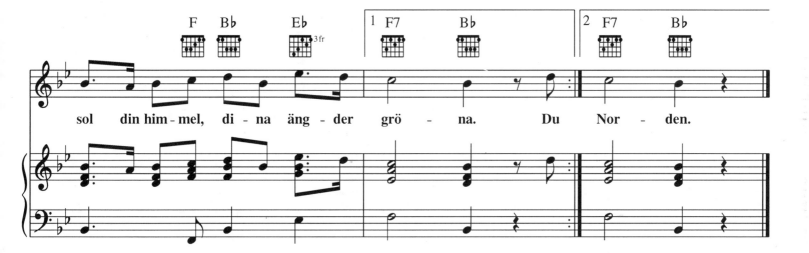

sol din him-mel, di-na äng-der grö - na. Du Nor - den.

Additional Lyrics

Du tronar på minnen från fornstora da'r,
Då ärat ditt namn flög över jorden.
Jag vet att du är och du blir, vad du var.
Ja, jag vill leva, jag vill dö i Norden,
Ja, jag vill leva, jag vill dö i Norden.

English Translation

1. Thou ancient, thou freeborn, thou mountainous North,
   In beauty and peace our hearts beguiling,
   I greet thee, thou loveliest land on the earth,
   Thy sun, thy skies, thy verdant meadows smiling,
   Thy sun, thy skies, thy verdant meadows smiling.

2. Thy throne rests on mem'ries from great days of yore,
   When worldwide renown was valour's guerdon.
   I know to thy name thou art true as before.
   Oh, I would live and I would die in Sweden.
   Oh, I would live and I would die in Sweden.

UGANDA
Pearl Of Africa

Words and Music by
GEORGE W. KAKOMA

Ai Ka - to - nda ffe tu - ku -
See additional lyrics

si - nza, Tu - wa - yo mu mi - ko - no gyo, E -

nsi ya - ttu, Fe - nnaa - wa - mu, E - nywe - ze -

bwe ng'O - lwaa - zi. Ai U -

Additional Lyrics

2. Ai Uganda! Oli muteefu,
   Abaana bo bakwagale,
   Bass'ekimu n'Ensi endala,
   Mu ddembe ne mu ssanyu.

3. Ai Uganda! Nyaff'Omulungi,
   Weyongerenga mu maaso,
   Tukwagale, Tukukuume,
   Ai Zaabu ya Afrika!

English Translation

1. Oh Uganda! May God uphold thee,
   We lay our future in thy hand.
   United, free;
   for liberty
   Together we'll always stand.

2. Oh Uganda! the land of freedom
   Our love and labour we give,
   And with neighbours all,
   At our country's call
   In peace and friendship we'll live.

3. Oh Uganda! the land that feeds us
   By sun and fertile soil grown,
   For our own dear land
   We'll always stand,
   The Pearl of Africa's Crown.

UKRAINE
Shche ne vmerla Ukrania

Words by PAUL CHUBÏNSKY
Music by MIKHAIL VERBÏTSKY

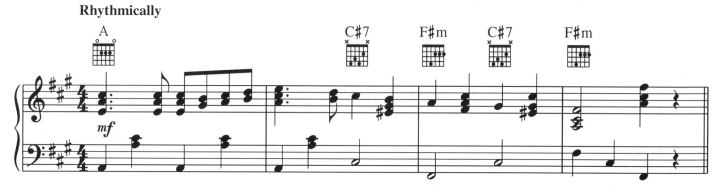

Rhythmically

Shche ne vmer - la U - kra - i - na, Ni sla - va, ni vo - la,

Shche nam brat - tia mo - lo - di - i U - smikh - net' - sia do - la:

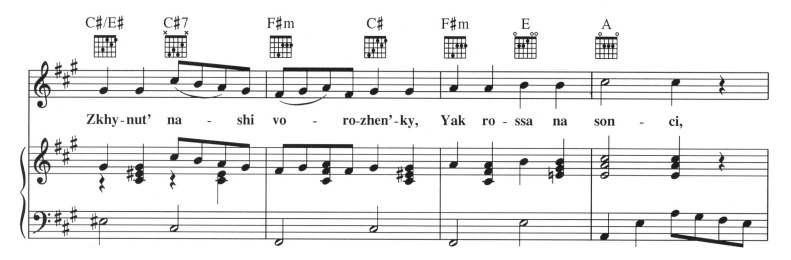

Zkhy - nut' na - shi vo - ro - zhen' - ky, Yak ro - ssa na son - ci,

English Translation

Ukraine has not died yet, brothers,
Neither fame nor freedom,
Destiny will smile yet brightly
Upon us, young kinsmen.

All our foes will surely perish
Like our dew under sunray,
We shall lord it, too, dear brother,
In our native country.

We lay down our soul and body
For freedom in battle,
And will prove that we are, brothers,
Men of Cossack mettle.

UNITED STATES OF AMERICA
The Star-Spangled Banner

Words by FRANCIS SCOTT KEY
Music by JOHN STAFFORD SMITH

1. O _____ say, can you see, by the dawn's ear - ly
2. shore dim - ly seen thro' the mists of the
3.,4. *(See additional lyrics)*

light, what so proud - ly we hail'd at the
deep, where the proud foe's haugh - ty host in dread

twi - light's last gleam - ing? Whose _ stripes and bright stars, thro' the
si - lence re - pos - es. What is that which the breeze, o'er the

Additional Lyrics

3. And where is the band who so dauntingly swore,
   'Mid the havoc of war and the battle's confusion.
   A home and a country they'd leave us no more?
   Their blood has wash'd out their foul footstep's pollution.
   No refuge could save the hireling and slave
   From the terror of flight or the gloom of the grave.
   And the star-spangled banner in triumph doth wave
   O'er the land of the free and the home of the brave.

4. O thus be it ever when free man shall stand,
   Between their loved homes and the war's desolation.
   Blest with vict'ry and peace, may the heav'n rescued land
   Praise the Power that hath made and preserved us a nation!
   Then conquer we must when our cause it is just,
   And this be our motto, "In God is our trust!"
   And the star-spangled banner in triumph shall wave
   O'er the land of the free and the home of the brave.

URUGUAY
¡Orientales, la patria o la tumba!

Words by FRANCISCO ACUÑA DE FIGUEROA
Music by FERNANDO QUIJANO and FRANCISCO JOSÉ DEBALLI

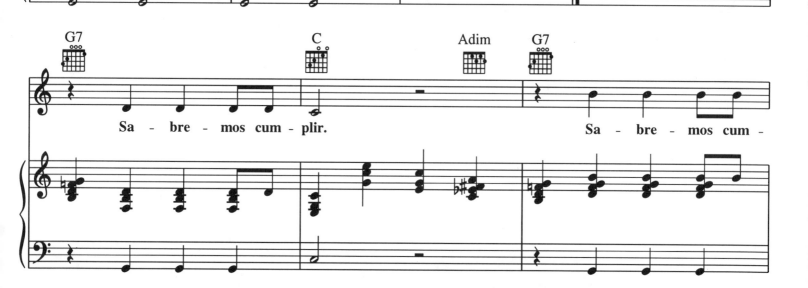

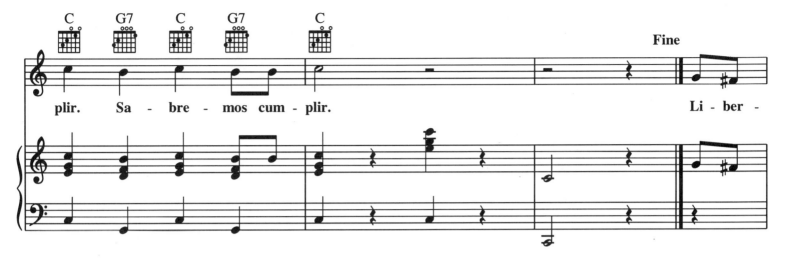

plir. Sa - bre - mos cum - plir.   Li - ber -

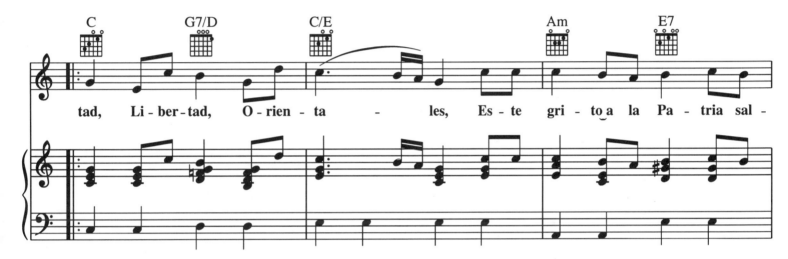

tad, Li - ber - tad, O - rien - ta - les, Es - te gri - to a la Pa - tria sal -

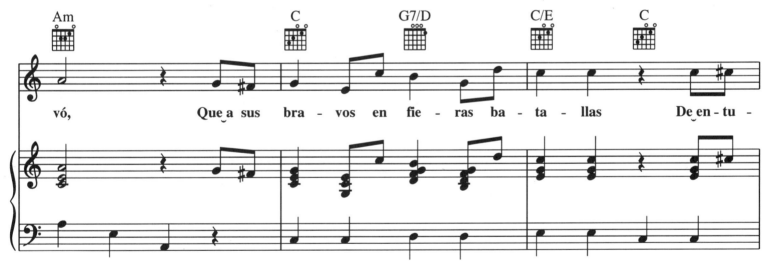

vó,   Que a sus bra - vos en fie - ras ba - ta - llas De en - tu -

sias - mo su - bli - me in - fla - mó.   Li - ber - mó.   De es - te

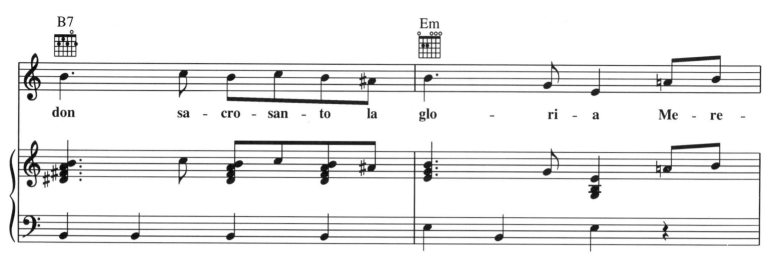

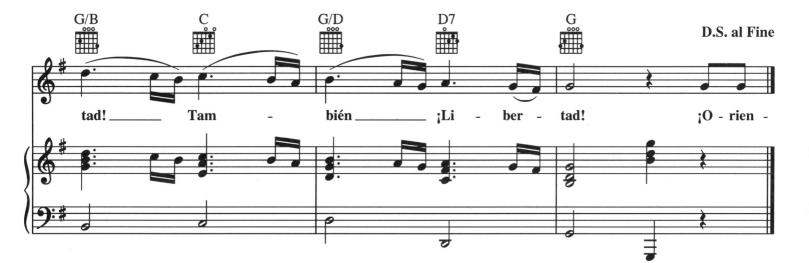

English Translation

People of Uruguay, unite or die!
Fight for freedom, or die in glory!
People of Uruguay, unite or die!
Fight for freedom, or die in glory!

This is our solemn vow,
And with heroism we will fulfill that vow.
This is our solemn vow,
And with heroism we will fulfill that vow.
We will fulfill that vow.
This is our solemn vow,
And with heroism we will fulfill that vow.
We will fulfill that vow.
We will fulfill that vow.
We will fulfill that vow.
We will fulfill that vow.

Freedom, oh freedom for Uruguay!
This is the cry of our nation.

The promise of sweet liberty
Will empower us in the bloodiest battles.
Freedom, oh freedom for Uruguay!
This is the cry of our nation.
The promise of sweet liberty
Will empower us in the bloodiest battles.

Our glorious country deserves this sacred freedom.
Tyrants, be gone! Tyrants, be gone! Tyrants, be gone!
"Freedom" will be our battle cry,
And it will be on our lips when we die.

"Freedom" will be our battle cry,
"Freedom" and "Freedom" again.
And "Freedom" again.
And "Freedom" again.

VIETNAM
Tiên quân ca

Words and Music by
VAN-CAO

English Translation

Soldiers of Vietnam, we go forward,
With the one will to save our Fatherland
Our hurried steps are sounding on the long and arduous road

Our flag, red with the blood of victory, bears the
spirit of our country
The distant rumbling of the guns mingles with our
marching song.
The path to glory passes over the bodies of our foes.
Overcoming all hardships, together we build our resistance bases.
Ceaselessly for the people's cause we struggle,
Hastening to the battlefield!
Forward! All together advancing!
Our Vietnam is strong eternal.

Soldiers of Vietnam, we go forward,
The gold star of our flag in the wind
Leading our people, our native land, out of misery
and suffering
Let us join our efforts in the fight for the building
of a new life.
Let us stand up and break our chains.
For too long have we swallowed our hatred
Let us keep ready for all sacrifices and our life will
be radiant.
Ceaselessly for the people's cause we struggle,
Hastening to the battlefield!
Forward! All together advancing!
Our Vietnam is strong eternal.

VENEZUELA
Gloria al bravo pueblo

Words by VINCENTE SALIAS
Music by JUAN JOSÉ LANDAETA

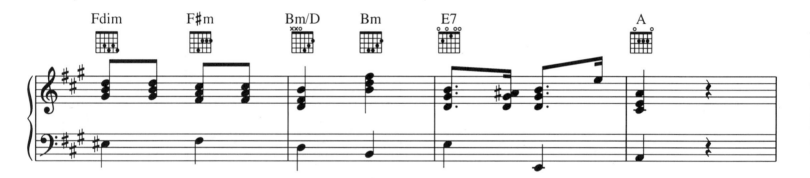

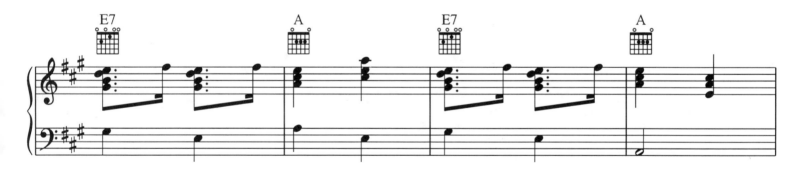

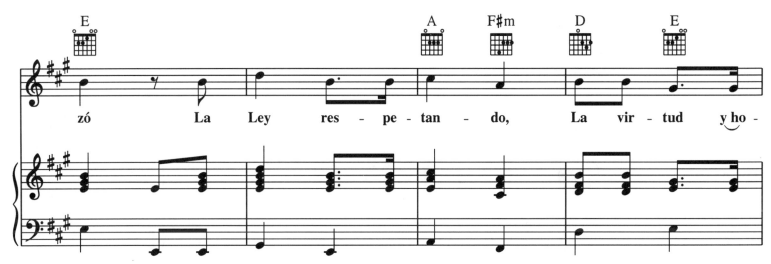

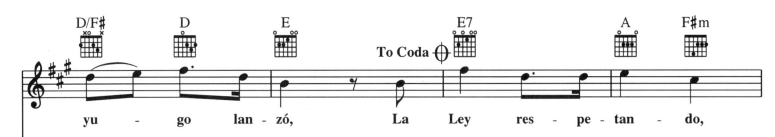

La vir - tud y ho - nor. ¡A - ba - jo ca - de - nas! ¡A - ba - jo ca -

de - nas! Gri - ta - ba el Se - ñor, Gri - ta - ba el Se - ñor, Y el

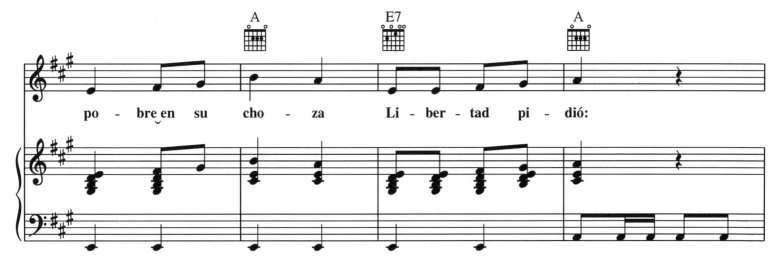

po - bre en su cho - za Li - ber - tad pi - dió:

A es - te san - to nom - bre Tem - bló de pa -

is - mo Que o - tra vez triun - fó.

Ley res - pe - tan - do, La vir - tud y ho - nor.

Additional Lyrics

Coro

2. Gritemos con brío:
Muera la opresión!
compatriotas fieles,
la fuerza es la unión;
y desde el Empíreo
el Supremo Autor,
un sublime aliento
al pueblo infundió.

Coro

3. Unida con lazos
que el cielo formó,
la América toda
existe en Nación;
y si el despotismo
levanta la voz,
seguid el ejemplo
que Caracas dió.

Coro

English Translation

Chorus   Glory to the brave people
that defeated the oppressor,
respecting the Law,
The virtue and honor.

1. Down with the chains!
Screamed the Lord;
and for the poor in his hut
Liberty was asked for:
To this Saint's name
the egotistic trembled
with fear that at another time
the oppressed would triumph.

Chorus

2. Let's scream with vigor:
Death to oppression!
loyal countrymen,
union is the force;
and from the Heavens above
the Supreme Author
instilled sublime courage
to the people.

Chorus

3. United with ties
that heaven created,
that all America exist
as a Nation;
and if the chaos
tries to raise its voice,
follow the example
that Caracas gave.

Chorus